# Nephew

# Nephew

A MEMOIR IN 4-PART HARMONY

MK Asante

**AMISTAD**

*An Imprint of* HarperCollins*Publishers*

Excerpts from *Buck: A Memoir* by MK Asante, published by Spiegel & Grau / Penguin Random House, 2013.

Lyrics from *The Nephew Soundtrack* from Wonderful Sound Studios appear courtesy of Nasir Hassan Allen Asante and Daahoud Jackson Asante.

Letters appear courtesy of Beverly Allen and Daahoud Jackson Asante.

HarperCollins books may be purchased for educational, business, or sales promotional use. For information, please email the Special Markets Department at SPsales@harpercollins.com.

FIRST EDITION

Library of Congress Cataloging-in-Publication Data

Names: Asante, Molefi K., 1981- author.
Title: Nephew: a memoir in four-part harmony / MK Asante.
Description: First edition. | New York: Amistad, [2023] | Includes bibliographical references.
Identifiers: LCCN 2023044260 (print) | LCCN 2023044261 (ebook) | ISBN 9780063275287 (hardcover) | ISBN 9780063275294 (trade paperback) | ISBN 9780063275300 (ebook)
Subjects: LCSH: Asante, Molefi K., 1981- | African Americans—Social conditions. | African Americans—Violence against. | African American families.
Classification: LCC E185.86 .A83 2023 (print) | LCC E185.86 (ebook) | DDC 362.88089/96073—dc23/eng/20231031
LC record available at https://lccn.loc.gov/2023044260
LC ebook record available at https://lccn.loc.gov/2023044261

24 25 26 27 28 LBC 5 4 3 2 1

I felt he found my letters
And read each one out loud

—Roberta Flack/Lauryn Hill
"Killing Me Softly"
1973/1996

# Contents

# 1 / Feel

Dear Nephew,

It's 3 AM. My veiny hands shake like leaves as I write you.

You're unconscious in the ICU at Temple University Hospital.

Rain streams outside, tears inside. The sky is off-black, the clouds are thick like blunt smoke, and the air is hot and heavy with pain. Shots. Screams. Moans. Blood. Piss. Smoke. Cries. Prayers. I can smell the stress.

You are nowhere near alone. I'm in the ER lobby with your mom, cousin Crystal, Big Tee, Bump, Grandma Beverly, and what feels like half of North Philly. Mounds of cheekbones, crescent lips, and scripture tattoos. I read "Only God Can Judge Me" on Bump's brick of a forearm. Your principal from the Crefeld School, George, is here too. Heartbroken and steely-eyed, he palms his forehead in utter shock and disbelief.

Detectives and blue jackets peak, prod, and circle like clocks. White coats with clipboards scramble in and out. Temple police in neon windbreakers stalk the hallways. Nurses *whoosh* by, scrubs striding in urgent purpose. Bloody sneaker prints stamp the hallway vinyl.

They don't let any of us go back to the trauma bays, not even your weeping mom. She snaps at the staff—

"I need to see him," she pleads with the front desk. She wears cornrows and an oversize black T-shirt that says "No Excuses"— the "o" is a weight plate and the "x" are two crisscross barbells.

The lady at the desk places a hand over her heart and shakes her head with sympathy. Her voice, stern. Her gaze, gentle but on point.

"I'm sorry, ma'am."

"Really? Y'all not going to let me go back there to see my son?!" Her thunderous mama bear voice cracks in heartbreak. Security surrounds the desk.

"Nikki, you have to let them do their job," Crystal says to your mom, rubbing her shoulders to calm her.

Your mom is what my mom, your grandmother (she prefers "Nna," which is Swahili for grandmother), calls a "textured woman." Nna describes a textured woman as a "woman with her hair plaited and then unplaited with the ripples remaining as she sashays from corner to throne."

Nna—who is just getting out of the hospital herself—wishes she could be here with you, too, but her illness, MSA (multiple systems atrophy), makes it too painful for her to travel. She says, after a life devoted to dance and movement, that she can't "count on her body anymore."

I'm leaning over the edge of this dingy hospital lobby chair repeating the same thing under heavy breath, "Fight! . . . Fight!" I accidently bite my bottom lip because I say "fight" with a hard, violent "f." Every time I say "fight," Tee adds, "Rumble that, Nephew!"

"Fight!" I can taste my blood.

"Rumble that, Nephew!"

"Fight!"

"Rumble that, Nephew!"

Tee saying "rumble" takes me back to freshmen year, on the battered blacktop at Fels High School when Calvin, a senior, called me out in front of the whole school, "Malo, you owe me a rumble." Of course, as a student of the sweet science, it also makes me think of that classic fight between Muhammad Ali and Sonny Liston when Ali says "Float like a butterfly, sting like a bee, ahhh! Rumble, young man, rumble, ahhh!" Back in the day I remember taking you to Joe Frazier's Gym on Broad Street, just a few blocks down from the hospital we're at now. We share a love for boxing; the art, the science, the sport, and all the Philly fighters like

Bernard "The Executioner" Hopkins, Steve "USS" Cunningham, and Jaron "Boots" Ennis. Boxing bonds us like fate.

Now I'm saying "Rumble that," too.

I think about one of my uncles, uncle Abdul, a former Golden Gloves champion. I remember when I was ten, he came to visit us in Philly all the way from Arizona. He showed me how to hold my hands.

*"Put your shit up," he says, putting his hands, like boulders, in front of his grill. He throws a jab at me. "Fuck you gon do, Nephew?" Sizing me up like a fitted hat. I jump out my seat.*

*"Gotta be ready for anything." Touches my chin with another jab. "C'mon now, put your shit up." I throw my hands up. He catches me again—bang. "Keep 'em up, young buck. Up! Protect yourself."*

*I move them up. His fist on my ribs. My hands fall like they're asleep. His fist on my chin. He picks me apart, then shows me how to hold my hands.*

*"Stand strong, feet shoulders' width apart, like this." Plants his feet, fixes my stance. "And if you ever want to kiss a ngh goodnight"—staring into his right fist—"swing it like this. Land it right there," he says, landing it slo-mo on my face.*

*I pull back and try to throw the same punch. "Like that?"*

*"Yup, just like that." Catching my punch. "That punch right there will make a ngh swallow and spit at the same damn time."*

I didn't know it at the time, but Uncle Abdul was preparing me to defend myself against bullies like Calvin.

Crystal is shattered stained glass. She paces in shards. Her prayers at three thousand degrees Fahrenheit and rising. Under stress, glass absorbs all of the energy of an impact and then releases that energy into a zillion tiny pieces. She explains that her and your uncle Tee have been at Temple from the get-go.

"We was here from the jump. It wasn't even a second that Nasir was by himself! Everything just happened so fast . . . But just as fast as it happened, though, we was on it," Crystal says. Her love for you is a concrete dam.

"No more than fifteen minutes," Tee adds, shaking his head and pressing his fingertips into his temples.

"Not even! As soon as I came down the block, the cops were like, 'We just sent everybody to Temple.' I busted that U-turn so fast . . ."

The shooting is on the news. The whole lobby watches Channel 6 in angst. They say you were one of nine teenagers—*nine!*—who were shot. Nine people shot is the definition of a mass shooting, but they don't call it that. They never call it that. Do you know why?

Silence grips the ER as the TV flashes a crime scene with yellow tape and numerical evidence markers on the ground.

"The magnitude," the anchor on TV says. "Nine people—eight men and a woman—between seventeen and twenty-five years old were shot on Twenty-Third Street near Huntingdon in North Philadelphia around 10:38 PM when two gunmen opened fire on as many as thirty people dancing at an outdoor graduation party on a warm Saturday. Some reportedly had been sharing photos and videos on social media. No arrests have been made . . ."

My heart free-falls. My own blood, shot in cold blood, in our "City of Brotherly Love." The city was literally named in love: "Phileo" means love in Greek and "adelphos" is brother. I feel the southern drawl of Bobby Blue Bland, whom they called "the Lion of the Blues," singing "Ain't No Love in the Heart of the City." Twenty-seven years after the original, Kanye West samples the Lion of the Blues—on a beat intended for DMX—on Jay-Z's "Heart of the City (Ain't No Love)."

**Look scrapper, I got nephews to look after
I'm not lookin' at you dudes, I'm lookin' past ya***

More bloody lines scroll across the screen in bold Helvetica: "Overnight Breaking" . . . "Quadruple Shooting" . . . "Man Shot, Killed in West Philadelphia" . . . "Multiple People Shot, 2 Dead After Violent Night in Philadelphia: Police"

Everything gets quiet—voices in the lobby, the TV, the noise in my head—when one of your doctors walks out to update your mom. Dr. Walker is narrow and monotone. His vibe: cold, numb. He updates us on your condition like an automated customer service robot. Tells us there are nine GSW's (gunshot wounds).

"Three in the right leg. One in the left leg. One on hip with bullet detained in back. Three shots on rear end. I imagine he ran."

"He ain't run!" Tee corrects him with the quickness. "He was shielding his little cousins from getting hit . . . and they didn't!"

---

* Jay-Z, "Heart of the City (Ain't No Love)," *The Blueprint*, 2001.

I nod in affirmation because that's the Nasir I know and love. That's my nephew: noble, selfless. You're the player on the basketball court who sacrifices their body to take a charge or dives to save the loose ball. Off the court, you're the kid who takes bullets for his little cousins. The kid who knows bullets don't have names on them.

"One GSW on the back right shoulder on surface. And one graze in the neck."

I'm sitting next to your grandma Beverly. Her salt-and-pepper crinkles kiss her tense collarbone.

"The spirit can hear," she tells me, sheen hands clasped into a steeple, nodding, as she whispers urgent prayers. I believe her. I pray in every language that God is called in and by every name that God is called upon.

"When they told me I had a brain tumor." She places a hand on me. Her touch is rich with life's jewels. I can feel my mom's favorite song, "Grandma's Hands"—*Hmm-mmh, Grandma's hands, picked me up each time I fell*—by Bill Withers, pulsing through her warm palms.

"My children were young then. I called on the Lord and said, 'Lord, I want to see my children grow up.'" She swipes a handkerchief from her purse and dabs at the shiny pools forming in the corners of her gaze. "I was thirty-six years old then . . . and I'll be seventy this year. Hezekiah! Hezekiah! . . ."

I can feel the high-powered spiritual energy emanating from her. I feel it everywhere like humidity. I can feel you, too.

You are the one who's shot, but I can feel the burning hollow tips piercing my body and shattering the storm windows to my spirit. Each blink is a hollering sting.

I have a condition they call mirror-touch synesthesia. Synesthesia is when people mix up their sensations; "hearing" colors, for example. Like Einstein once said, "I often think in music." The mirror-touch form of synesthesia is the feeling of sensations of others. You feel it—I feel it. Feel me?

# 2 / The North Star

I'm in North Carolina when the shooting happens. As soon as I get the call from your mom—she can barely squeeze the words out: "Nasir . . . was . . . shot"—I'm out. I jump in the car—the same Range Rover Autobiography that I taught you to drive in—and hit I-95 North to come to Philly. I spark a fronto of sativa and vroom up under moonlight and over drill beats.

I pass a huge Confederate flag propped up between Quantico and Fredericksburg, Virginia. It's lit up from below and flails in the wind like a ghost. Trees sway. Virginia is the birthplace of the slavery nightmare in America. Blood on the leaves. I press on. Eyes on the prize.

On my midnight race up to Philly from North Carolina, I listen to all of your music. Rhythm rushes. Your frequencies fill the fast night air.

I catch glimpses of your song titles as they flash and glow on my dashboard: "Strangers," "Casket," "Prosper," "True Story," "4or Real," "Once Again," "Cold Nights," "Homicide," "Youngin," "Ain't Just Rap," "Pray 4 Philly," "Karma," "Hashtag," "Be Me," . . .

It's fucked up when you give out love
And you don't even get it back
Came from the jungle with killers
I hopped off that porch and had to adapt[*]

I always do this—spit lyrics under my breath—all day, every day. The lyrics that resonate with me the most always leak out, like the truth does.

Your beats vibrate my essence and snap my head back and forth like whiplash. They thump through me. Your autobiographical bars send shivers straight down my spine. Your lyrics illustrate your journey. I remember the "jungle with killers" and the moment when you "hopped off that porch."

The drive from Chapel Hill is six hours at one hundred miles per hour, which feels more like fifty in the supercharged V8. I struggle to settle in for the long ride, sweaty palms gripping and regripping the woodgrain wheel, as it starts to sink in.

When I listen to you sing and flow on your song "Prosper," it inspires a sense of hope for your current situation. "Prosper" is the inflatable life raft fighting against violent rip currents. Poet Emily Dickinson, aka the New England Mystic, once wrote: "Hope is the thing with feathers - / That perches in the soul - / And sings the tune without the words - / And never stops - at all." My hope is that someday you will be able to hear this "tune," so I must keep writing, feeling, and believing, because to write, right now, is to feel, and feeling is believing.

---

[*]  Neph, "Strangers," *The Nephew Soundtrack*, 2024.

Although you are in critical condition, "Prosper" pushes me to remember that beautiful "thing with feathers" that carried us this far. I think about how music, one of the things you do so well, possesses the power to heal. In ancient Egypt, the harp is used in healing temples. Modern scientific studies reveal that the vibrations from music can lower blood pressure, reduce heart rate, relieve anxiety and pain, and bring about an overall sense of peace to the listener. In ancient Greece, the god Apollo is not only the god of medicine, he is the god of music as well. They build music-filled temples to harmonize the body.

> No weapon, formed, against me
> Shall prosper, it won't work
> Yeah you know I'm from the dirt
> Had to go for days, same shirt*

You harmonize from the book of Isaiah (54:17) with the depth and soul of a big-boned gospel singer from the deep South. Someone like Muddy Waters from Rolling Fork, Mississippi, or Odetta from Birmingham, Alabama. Or a young Aretha Franklin at New Bethel Baptist Church in Detroit, Michigan. I remember you playing the drums, backed by handclaps and church-shoe stomps, at Grandma Beverly's Macedonia Free Will Baptist Church in North Philly. That's my first glimpse at your ancestral rhythm and impeccable time.

Your drumming pulsates through the wooden pews and stained glass of Macedonia and pours out onto the corner of Twenty-First and Cecil B. Moore Avenue. Your drum is a voice that speaks our mother tongue, sending messages and warnings. Back in the day,

---

* Neph, "Prosper," *The Nephew Soundtrack*, 2024.

the moment white Southern enslavers realize that Africans are not simply *playing* drums, but *speaking* drums to communicate, they criminalize our percussion. They actually ban our drums, outlaw our beats, spouting BS like:

> "It is absolutely necessary to the safety of this Province, that all due care be taken to restrain Negroes from using or keeping of drums, which may call together or give sign or notice to one another of their wicked designs and purposes."
>
> —Slave Code of South Carolina, Article 36 (1740)

See, Nephew, the enslavers didn't realize that we are born on-beat, and that, just like the will to be free, it's embedded in us, drum or no drum. This is why the jazz pianist Randy Weston, who is from Nna's neighborhood in Brooklyn, says "your heartbeat is your drum, your voice is your sound—and music is supposed to put you in tune with nature."

Your voice is the drum they fear. Your voice is freedom—it's *Uhuru*!

> Misinterpret my level of genius and call it cuckoo
> But the Swahili meaning of freedom is still uhuru*

Weston's first album is called *Uhuru Afrika* and the liberation music he recorded in 1961 is still relevant today. The album has

---

\* Black Thought, "State Prisoner," *Streams of Thought, Vol. 3: Cane & Able*, 2019.

two songs featuring bars from Harlem Renaissance poet Langston Hughes.

> Africa, where the great Congo flows!
> Africa, where the whole jungle knows
> A new dawning breaks, Africa!
> A young nation awakes, Africa!
> The freedom wind blows!*

I feel that Uhuru freedom "wind" blowing when I listen to "Water"—your modern rap remake of the spiritual "Wade in the Water"—as well as the drums from Macedonia Free Will Baptist sewn into your Philly rasp.

> Mama tried to tell me about that water
> Said "little boy watch that water"
> And she warned me to hop out that water
> Cause ain't no love in that water†

Your use of "water" as a metaphor—for trouble, for destructive "wet" blunts dipped in PCP-laced embalming fluid, and for the streets—is deep because that's the essence of the original song. More than a song, "Wade in the Water," just like our drums they banned, is a coded message. During their daring escapes from the hell of slavery, our ancestors would sing "Wade in the Water" to

---

* Randy Weston featuring Langston Hughes, "Introduction: Uhuru Kwanza," *Afrika Uhuru*, 1961.
† Neph, "Water," *The Nephew Soundtrack*, 2024.

signal runaways to get off the trail and into the water to avoid being
sniffed out by bloodhounds.

> Wade in the water,
> Wade in the water, children,
> Wade in the water
> God's gonna trouble the water*

Most Black spirituals are codes and odes to freedom. Singing
"Follow the Drinking Gourd" is code for the Big Dipper (it looks
like a drinking gourd), which points to the North Star. "Steal Away
to Jesus" is code for an upcoming escape plan. "Sweet Chariot" is
code for the underground railroad. All of our songs are codes.

Escapes, rebellions, and freedom are all encoded in our music.
Frederick Douglass, who escaped slavery in Maryland, writes that
in our music, "every tone was a testimony against slavery, and a
prayer to God for deliverance from chains." In his 1903 book,
*The Souls of Black Folk*, W.E.B. Du Bois writes that our music is
our "greatest gift," describing our songs as "the singular spiritual
heritage of the nation." We still carry this tradition of freedom
in hip-hop today. Think about Jay-Z's book *Decoded*, in which he
writes, "A poet's mission is to make words do more work than they
normally do, to make them work on more than one level."

Nephew, your lyrics operate on more than one level too,
continuing the code-carrying tradition. I barrel down a barren

---

* Jubilee Fisk Singers, "Wade in the Water," *New Jubilee Songs as Sung by the Fisk
Jubilee Singers*, 1901.

highway, listening for your codes now, hanging on every word—
"Glock" ... "demons" ... "pressure" ... "bottom" ... "struggle" ...
"vent" ... "pain" ... "Lord" ... "recognize" ... "independent" ...
"Rasta" ... "ambulance" ... "party" ... "cutoff" ... "grind" ...
"homicide" ... "trenches" ... "tears" ... "impossible"—looking for
clues, searching for answers.

> Gotta get it,
> I'm tryna touch a dollar
> From the trenches
> I ain't never have a father.*

Your line—"I ain't never have a father"—hits me quick and hard
like a stiff Money Mayweather jab.

My mind zooms to last month, when we were together, down in
North Carolina. The big night sky is a clear, shimmery black. You
look up at the stars gazing down on us.

"I almost forgot they were even up there," you tell me. "Hard to
see them jawns in Philly."

I wonder—if the city can make you forget about the stars, I
wonder what else can it make you forget about?

"That kind of light pollution is called sky glow," I say. "It's never
truly *dark* dark." And maybe that's why the city never sleeps?

---

* Neph, "Trap," *The Nephew Soundtrack*, 2024.

"See that star right there?" I point.

"Yea."

"That's the North Star. Two thousand times brighter than our sun. It's the only star in the constellation that doesn't travel across the sky. Stays put—always points north. Our ancestors used that star as a guide when they were escaping these . . ." I survey the surrounding acres, mature trees, babbling brook. "Plantations all around here." I mean, it *is* North Carolina, I always remind myself. Then I recall hearing a clip of Malcolm X, who during his introduction of Mississippi native Fannie Lou Hamer, put it like this: "Some people wonder, well, what has Mississippi got to do with Harlem? It isn't actually Mississippi; it's America. America is Mississippi. There's no such thing as a Mason-Dixon Line—it's America. There's no such thing as the South—it's America."

**They search the web to ride waves and stuff**
**We search the Atlantic for enslaved who jumped***

It *is* America. Specifically, we're in Chapel Hill, North Carolina, nicknamed the Southern Part of Heaven. Chapel Hill is the birthplace of George Moses Horton, a remarkable man and poet who was born enslaved in 1798. As a kid, Horton breaks the law by teaching himself how to read and write. I can remember, as a senior in high school, when I first started seriously reading. A light bulb goes off in my head, I reflect:

---

* MK Asante, "Mudcloth," *The Nephew Soundtrack*, 2024.

*Now I see why reading was illegal for Black people during slavery.*
*I discover that I think in words. The more words I know, the more*
*things I can think about. . . . Reading was illegal because if you*
*limit someone's vocab, you limit their thoughts. They can't even*
*think of freedom because they don't have the language to.*

By the age of twenty, Horton is walking to the campus of the
University of North Carolina at Chapel Hill to sell poetry for
seventy-five cents a pop. Love poems, death poems, religious
poems, he becomes the go-to poet in Chapel Hill. He uses the
money to publish his first book, *The Hope of Liberty* (1829), all
while still enslaved! It reminds me of when I read Assata Shakur's
autobiography, *Assata*, which was written over a hundred years
after *The Hope of Liberty*. Assata writes, "People get used to anything.
The less you think about your oppression, the more your
tolerance for it grows. After a while, people just think oppression
is the normal state of things. But to become free, you have to be
acutely aware of being a slave."

Horton never got "used to oppression" and never lost sight of
his mission to "become free." He leveraged the success of his first
book to publish two more books: *The Poetical Works of George M.
Horton, The Colored Bard of North Carolina* and *Naked Genius*. With
three books under his belt, Horton then used his book money
to purchase his freedom. A free man, Horton left Chapel Hill
and headed north where he settled in Philly (of course). Horton
eventually left Philly after two decades and sailed to Liberia,
Africa, his final resting place—home. There's a historical landmark
plaque right down the road from me in Pittsboro, North Carolina,
on US 15/501, which reads:

## GEORGE MOSES HORTON

### ca. 1798–1883

Slave poet. His *The Hope of Liberty* (1829) was first book by
a Black author in South. Lived on farm 2 mi. SE.


Horton's poetry is the North Star that delivered his freedom.

"God's time is always near. He set the North Star in the
heavens," says Harriet Tubman. "He gave me the strength in my
limbs; He meant I should be free." Tubman, who, like Horton, lived
in Philly for a period of time, freed hundreds of enslaved Africans,
and famously said that she could have freed thousands "if only they
knew they were slaves." I can hear the heavy voices of Tubman,
Horton, and Assata in concert.

In Chapel Hill, we go to the same UNC Chapel Hill campus that
Horton made famous. I take you to eat at Sup Dogs, the sports bar
with murals of Michael Jordan and J. Cole painted inside. They're
not the massive, vibrant murals we see daily in Philly, but at least
they illustrate the impact of Black North Carolinians. I remember
us sitting outside on Franklin Street, the quintessential college strip.
Headlights and LED signs illuminate our table. Your strong, defined
face is the color of black walnuts. You lean into our convo, fully
present. Your arms are long and muscular like a wide receiver's.

With steady, radiant eyes, you hand me a scratched-up Sony
thumb drive and tilt your Phillies "P" hat up and off to the side.

"Let me know what you think Unc," you say, real cool, but with
active volcanoes in your eyes. It's a familiar fire and I feel your
passion in the flash.

"It's an honor, Nephew." I slip the drive in my denim and dap you up.

"Oh yeah, I was wondering . . ." your eyes drift down for a moment then lock with mine. "What's up with my dad?"

I think to myself, *damn, look at the size of this kid's heart!* To ask about a man—my brother, your dad—whom you have never met, is a testament to your character. Lionheart.

It's the first time you ask about him in years. As a little kid, you asked me innocent questions like "Do you know my dad?" and "Where does my dad live?" But as soon as you *"hopped off that porch"* on Lehigh Avenue at thirteen, you never asked again.

**Growing up, you had an option, me and my nghs didn't**
**Pop missing so I start pot whipping**[*]

Stiff Money Mayweather jabs turn into ruthless Iron Mike Tyson uppercuts ("It's ludicrous!").

Your heart gets even bigger when you tell me, "It's for Nna."

"For Nna?" I'm a little lost.

You explain to me that when we visited Nna's house earlier that day, she pulled you to the side. She tells you that her health is suffering, and she doesn't know how much longer she has to live.

---

[*]  Neph, "Wat Ya Life Like," *The Nephew Soundtrack*, 2024.

She tells you that she is proud of you and your music but doesn't like when you refer to women as "b's and hoes." She encourages you to expand your vocabulary and, before you go "calling women out of their names," think about the strong women in your life, the textured ones who raised and nurtured you; the ones who fill the hospital now.

Lastly, she tells you that she will not be able to die in peace or rest in peace until you and your dad connect—that's her North Star.

# 3 / Back in Blood

I apologize for not answering your questions about your music and your dad right away that night. And now, as I listen to your catalog of music, searching for answers about who shot you and why, I realize you've been searching for answers your whole life.

> Only the real can understand
> Tryna count up the bands
> Tryna provide for the fam
> Ain't doing that—you ain't a man*

Your search for answers leads you to hug Philly back blocks that don't hug back and to jump into the same seductive streets that swallowed your dad . . . and his dad. This is not a story that you know yet, but should, because our family cannot afford the high costs of secrets.

> Been through the mud, rain, pain,
> Whatever you name, we ain't the same†

---

* Neph, "Eat," *The Nephew Soundtrack*, 2024.
† Neph, "Hard in the Trap," *The Nephew Soundtrack*, 2024.

In our family, we are born into a pulsing cycle of secrets. When I was a teenager, Nna tells me that our old house in East Oak Lane was a "shelter of secrets." She writes about it in her journal.

*Our world is a secret . . . MK's nightly forays into the streets, his father's nightly forays at the office or out of town and my nightly forays forgetting, escaping, and wishing pain away. My soul and heart are in flight. I am looking for me. I am looking for the "me" that I lost somewhere along the way. Morning has come . . . and I am pretending to be asleep. My oldest son is away, and my home has become the house of secrets.*

Shattering the cycle of secrets in our family is poetic justice.

Your search for answers also leads you home to poetry. I hear the poetry punching through your verses. I can see the poem in you. I see you as a poem. In his book *Decoded*, Jay-Z writes, "Rap is poetry, and a good MC is a good poet, you can't just half-listen to a song once and think you've got it." On my six-hour drive to Philly from Chapel Hill, I listen to your tracks on repeat, catching something new in the poetry each time.

Poetry runs through your blood like plasma. Your dad, Uzi, despite any shortcomings, is a bona fide lyrical genius. Even though he's never officially released any music or pursued a career in rap, he is a real MC (master of ceremonies). Uzi's fixed in my top five, dead or alive, greatest MC's ever. When he opens his mouth, his bass commands the attention of any cipher. His voice is charged, deep, and unpredictable, like an electric bass guitar. He's your favorite rapper's favorite rapper. A local underrated Philly GOAT, Uzi is among the best to ever put pen to pad. Cut from the same cloth as the African Griots, who tell epic stories through music, Uzi is a complex, brilliant, and poetic soul serving up bars of fire (a *bar*tender). He is Uptown's Vodka (1,000 proof) or Southwest Philly's Spittage (RIP) on the *2 Raw For The Streets* DVDs. He is Gil Scott-Heron before the drugs—and after the drugs, singing, "the revolution will not be televised," or "man is a complex being: he makes deserts bloom—and lakes die."

I hear the griots in you, too. You are Young Gunz' Young Chris in a dark room at Hot 97, holding it down for Neef, creating a new blueprint from *Gratz straight to the Roc like Darius Miles* . . . ("He's sixteen!"). You are a hungry teenage Meek Mill—Dickies suit and fuzzy braids—on Berks Street, spitting straight flames into the Major Films DVD lens.

> With my brothers in double sole butters
> Why you hating when don't a single soul love us?
> No prayer answered, can't believe in something above us
> Rap sheet, we don't know they undercovers*

As a lyricist, your dad is a poet and a rapper. This is remarkable because all rap is not poetry in the same way that all noise is not music. Anyone can rap, but the "poet," as musician, filmmaker, and poet Saul Williams says, "is the one who realizes that their vulnerability is their power . . . the poet finds strength in exposing their humanity, their vulnerability, thus making it possible for us to find connection and strength through their work." Your vulnerability isn't a weakness, it's one of your superpowers.

---

\* Uzi, "Open Bar," *The Nephew Soundtrack*, 2024.

Poetry pumps through Uzi's blood, your blood, and my blood through our Brooklyn matriarch, Nna. Nna, too, is a poet. Her poetry, like yours, is autobiographical and cloaked in code. "My poetry," she tells me, her hands in motion like magic wands in sync with her words, "is about where we've been, where we find ourselves now, and where we are going." Nna is the bridge, our very own Golden Gate, between the *no longer* and the *not yet*.

Nna starts her poetic journey in the sixties during BAM (the Black Arts Movement). BAM is like the artistic little sister of the Black Power Movement. Growing up, BAM poets like Sonia Sanchez—who reveals that her purpose as a writer is "to keep in contact with our ancestors and to spread truth to people"—come to chill at our house in East Oak Lane, or "Smoke Lane," as Uzi always calls it.

> We fucked, all stuck in the hood—broke engine
> Only work is in Grandma old kitchen*

In 1978, when Uzi is four years old, Nna pens a poem called "Stories My Grandmother Would Have Told Me," about what wasn't passed down to her.

> My grandmother would have
>         told me about
> Anokye and Nat Turner
>         but she couldn't
> My grandmother would have
>         told me about Mzilikazi and Chaka

---

* Uzi, "Open Bar," *The Nephew Soundtrack*, 2024.

but she never got the chance
My grandmother would have
        told me about Toussaint and Tubman
        but she didn't know about them

Nna's grandmother didn't teach her about Anokye, the high
priest of the Asante empire in Ghana (where our last name, Asante,
comes from); or about Nat Turner leading the biggest, bloodiest
slave rebellion in US history; or about Mzilikazi, the African king
who founded Zimbabwe; or Chaka Zulu, the South African warrior
who was known as "the battle-ax that excels over other battle-axes in
sharpness"; or Harriet Tubman, aka Moses, who frees herself and over
three hundred other people from the evil shackles of enslavement.

Nna mentions these names in her poem with great purpose:
to teach us, to pass on to us, what her grandmother didn't pass on,
couldn't pass on, to her. To show us who we were, who we are, and
who we can become.

My grandmother would have
        told me stories
that could lull me to sleep
        and wake me up with
some kind of direction
Hard to imagine
        Grandma telling me
any stories though
when Grandma lived the
only story she knew
        and she really didn't
        care to tell that one

The tragedy of secrets is the blindness they perpetuate. When we keep them, we don't learn from our history—global, national, or familial— and we end up repeating avoidable mistakes and failing to learn the touch and texture of the extraordinary cloth from which we're cut.

My grandmother should have
told me
a story that would have
freed me and her
and we would have flown
to Jupiter
and made believe
that grandmothers and their
children and their children
are something special
no matter what their color be
and if America don't know it
then Jupiter does!

Nna says that everything—secrets, lies, and truths—"comes out in the wash." And that in our family, the wash is our letters. In our family, letters travel generations.

This letter is the answer to both of your questions about your music (*let me know what you think, Unc?*) and about your dad (*what's up with my dad?*).

# 4 / Kites

Letters are a part of our family DNA, braided into our chromosomes like Senegalese two-strand twists.

There are two letters I've received in my life that I will cherish forever. The first letter is from Uzi. I'm like ten or eleven and he inks a letter from jail in Arizona. I'm playing outside with my best friends who live next door, twin brothers Sam and Andy, or as my mom calls them, "the Grannums." Sam and Andy's parents are both pastors, Bishop Dr. C. Milton Grannum and Rev. Dr. Hyacinth Bobb-Grannum, and Nna calls them "a real class act." Sometimes Nna goes next door and prays with the Grannums, a prayer for their sons. My prayer is simple: "Free Uzi!"

I remember the bliss I felt when Nna handed me the letter. I peeped his inmate number on the envelope and ripped it open. Reading his words, I felt his deep voice like he's in my room over Dolby Digital 5.1 Surround Sound:

January 9, 1994

Malo,

Wassup man? Hope everything is good with you yo. I'm in this hell hole wondering my fate. When they transferred me here I wasn't 18 yet so I was on the 7th floor, where the other minors that have been transferred as adults are housed. We stayed in our cells 23 and 1, meaning we were in our cells for 23 hours a day and one hour out to take a shower and make a phone call. That shit makes u crazy, u find yourself thinking out loud, standing at your door for hours on end watching the guards watch you. I've read the whole Bible like 5 times cover to cover . . . "Psalms" is cool, keeps me calm. I'm still trying to get a *Koran*, but u know, this is Arizona! haha. I can tell the fuckin time just by the way the sun hits my cell through my sun slit which pretends to be a window . . . just by the shadows it casts on my cell walls. I'm on some monk shit.

I still can't get used to the constant noise in here man, it's something I can't explain, it's a fucking roar, a constant roar, like hard wind blowing in your ear all the time, u don't forget about it. People never stop talking, yelling or screaming in here. I kind of think of it like how a black hole would sound, cuz this place is a void—a fucking hum of pain.

The kids in there had done some serious shit, mostly murder though. I used to think that a killer was a certain type of person. I now know that killing is an emotional reaction, cuz most killers aren't crazy people, shit is crazy.

The kid next door to me was an ese named Pelon, he's in here for murder, and attempted murder. He is in a gang outta phoenix called Duppa Villa, his dad is in it, his mom is in it, this shit is like a rites of passage to the ese's, they take this shit in stride. When I first got here he gave me some food. Uncle John said in prison don't accept nothing from nobody, but fuck that I was hungry! It was a Snickers bar and a bag of Corn Nuts, maaan that shit made me feel like I wasn't in jail anymore—just seeing the wrappers! Ain't that some shit? He sent it on a "kite" string. That's a long ass rope made from sock thread and boxer-short elastic, that's how we send shit from cell to cell, letters, food, and other shit like that. When the guards see u doing it they take ya string from u, motha-fukas go crazy when they get their strings took, it's like losing ya house phone!

On my 18th birthday, midnight, three guards came to take me downstairs to the main jail general population. The muhfuka told me "happy birthday kid, welcome to hell" . . . The day before Pelon passed off a shank to me made out of paper—yes paper!—the shit is hard as metal and the shit has a spear point on it! Paper yo! He told me they like to fuck with us young BUCKS cuz we're small and shit, he said if a punto fucks with me bang 'em in the stomach right where the navel is. I feel that, but I just want to go home, but I guess I gotta do what I gotta do yo.

Man, one thing I learned in here is that killas can be punks and punks can be killas, it don't matter. Just stand your square, never retreat—fuck that! If somebody wants to steal my respect, they gotta pay in blood dog.

Pain is weakness leaving the body, Malo, remember that.

So yeah I'm in GP now with the adults, been here for a minute. They got me in the maximum security block, red card status, it's better than the 7th floor shit though. At least I can play ball, walk around, have some real human contact, and watch TV.

Out here on the West Coast they gangbang crazy, shit goes down everyday, these mothafukas take the shit seriously. My cellie is my boy B-Brazy, he's a blood from Mad Swan Blood Gang. We look out for each other, the ngh is down as shit. Check this: he never uses the letter C! when he talks he replaces the letter C with B, and when he writes he crosses out the letter C and anything else that reminds him of Crips! hahahaha. There are like 10 Crips for every Blood, so Bloods be ridin hard with each other, cuz they r outnumbered, so because I roll with Brazy, I'm what they call Bulletproof, 80 Proof, and Shotgun, meaning not Blood, but bangs with Blood . . . fuck it!

Uncle Abdul said I'll probably do 5 years, I guess I can live with that, It's better than the 25 years the public defender told me I was facing when I was in juvie! I know one thing, the boy in me has died, I've been forced to be a man. Mom and dad can't help me in here, nobody gives a fuck about Afrocentricity or African dance in this joint, for real!

Malo, don't ever come to a place like this, it breeds violence, hate, and ignorance, and u never relax, u always have to watch what goes on around you, every little gesture, every word can be the difference between chilling or getting ya face tore off man . . . it's fucked up. It will change your "eyes"—do u get that? Ya spirit changes. The next time mom sees me, she won't see her baby looking back at her, she will see someone else, someone different.

I've had a couple run ins since I've been in here. I got into it with this OG Crip dude named Cisco Kaddafi. We were playing ball and the mothafuka kept hacking me. I got tired of it, and I threw my hands up at him. He told me "not here, we gonna do this at the "house," which is our word for the cell block. Brazy told me to "soap" him, which means take bars of soap and put them in a sock as a weapon, shit does damage yo.

When we got back to the house, I b-lined for my hut, but he came to my door and said "naw lil loc we gonna do this like G'z, ain't gonna be no weapons", at that point I had to man up. We went to the showers and I just started swinging. Cisco is like 6'2, 250, but I was connecting! He grabbed me though and slammed the shit outta me, but I got right the fuck back up. By then the guard rushed in and choked us out on their SWAT team bullshit. They kept asking me if he attacked me, cuz he is known for shit like that. I was like "fuck no! I attacked him!" even though it wasn't exactly like that. haha. They wanted to know if I wanted to transfer to another cell block, or did I fear for my safety . . . what? Fuck no! . . . I'm not a bitch, and I'm not gonna have a bitch jacket following me . . . in here u don't go out like that, even if it's not in ya best personal interest. They let me back in the pod, and I was chillin. Cisco called me up to his cell, and was like "yo homie I like ya heart" and he shook my hand. Then he gave two "tailor mades" which is a full cigarette, it's like giving someone 10 bucks.

See Malo? Stand your square . . . Nghz respect u for that shit, no matter what! If u want my stripes, they not Velcro, u gotta rip my arm off to get them . . . yahmeen!

I'm still writing my RHYMEs (Rap Hard Your Money Equal) though, I got this crazy ass song called "24 Hours." The hook goes:

24 hours anotha soul loses power
some bring sun rays, some dark days and showers

some never see they visions so believe u blessed
life is just a test u got the right to be stressed

But Malo, on some real shit, I wish I could go back to 707 and being a kid again, chillin in my room doing card tricks and chillin wit Ted . . . u know? I wish me and u could rewind and play hanger ball in my room, or tracker with Akil and Ahmed in the yard.

I've seen and heard too much yo, it'll never be the same.

Think about the shit u do Malo, don't dick ride nobody, be yourself, and fuck drugs. Weed ain't a drug, though, it's spiritual stimuli . . . haha.

Protect mom, pray for me, and sooner or later we will unite again . . . We r the last Asantes ngh, we gotta keep this shit alive . . .

This is the only letter Uzi ever sends me from Arizona and I cherish it. I read, re-read it, and repeat like I'm studying it for a test (Uzi's last line from "24 Hours"—*life is just a test u got the right to be stressed*—jumps out like 3-D).

Nna writes letters to Carole (herself), which is what her name was before she changed it to Kariamu. She says she writes to Carole "as a way of relieving the tension and memories." As a teenager, I secretly read her journal. "Letters to Carole," it says on the front. I remember thinking: The journal is heavy to be so little. Does ink weigh that much? Can ink weigh that much? How can ink weigh that much?

Your grandfather Bob writes letters to God—to God!—for an entire year, in 1971, and then to Nna from jail in 1972. (*Dear God, strange things are happening to me.*)

And your great grandmother, Ruth, Nna's mom, who usually keeps things close to the vest, writes your grandfather Bob a letter when he's incarcerated. In jail, a letter, or a "kite," as the bros call it, is a gift from God.

Neither bars nor bullets can stop love letters. I share our words with you now so that you may learn, grow, connect, elevate, and heal.

All of our voices—Uzi's bass, Bob's tenor, my alto, and Nna's soprano—reach you now, in four-part harmony.

# 5 / Their Eyes Were Watching God

It's actually not your grandfather, Uzi, or Nna's letters that spark *this* letter—it's actually yours. This letter starts with your letter. You are the spark.

You may not remember this, but at just five years old, you wrote a letter to your dad. You wrote the letter in 2005, a week after Hurricane Katrina battered the Gulf Coast, the levees broke, and New Orleans sank.

Your mom didn't even know about the letter. Your grandma Beverly, who is now leading a prayer circle in the middle of the ER lobby, enclosed your letter within her own letter to my brother.

Grandma Beverly's prayers drown out the incessant hum of despair in the ER. "Will He do it?" she asks. A chorus of mmhmm's and uh-huh's come back.

You wrote your letter on the same day that Kanye West, during a live NBC telethon for the victims of Katrina, went off script and said, "I hate the way they portray us in the media . . . If you see a Black family, it says they're looting. If you see a white family, it says they're searching for food." He ends by calling out FEMA and President

Bush for their lack of response to the tragedy, looking straight into the camera and declaring "George Bush doesn't care about Black people."

"Go and tell Hezekiah!" Grandma Beverly shouts. "This is what the Lord God of your ancestor David says: I have heard your prayer; I have seen your tears . . ."

The Katrina tragedy—specifically all of the people who couldn't afford the luxury of evacuation—reminds me of the devasting hurricane in Zora Neale Hurston's 1937 novel, *Their Eyes Were Watching God*. Hurston, who went to high school at Morgan College (now Morgan State University) and college at Howard University, wrote vividly about the storm: "The wind came back with triple fury, and put out the light for the last time. They sat in company with the others in other shanties, their eyes straining against crude walls and their souls asking if He meant to measure their puny might against His. They seemed to be staring at the dark, but their eyes were watching God."

Grandma Beverly sends your letter, along with hers, to Nna's house since she didn't have Uzi's address.

September 2, 2005

Dear Daahoud (Uzi):

You don't know me, but I feel like I know you. You see I have been praying for you since you became a part of my family. When you came together with my daughter and made my beautiful grandson you made yourself a part of my family. The word of God says that children are a gift from God, and Nasir is a true gift from God. Your son is handsome, has a beautiful personality, compassionate, intelligent, respectful and talented, and even though he said something that let me know he is hurting because you are not a part of his life, he still laughs all the time.

One day I had your son, Nasir, and his cousin, my other grandson, Trey, and I kept getting their names mixed up. We had been out for quite some time and I said to someone that Nasir's mom and dad are going to be wondering where their son is, but I mean to say Trey. Nasir looked up at me with his big brown innocent eyes and said, "I don't have a daddy." I could feel his pain. This is why I am writing you this letter because although my daughter is doing a great job taking care of her child, she can't be a mother and a father. As long as you are not in his life there will always be something missing in his heart and life, and it will be you. God gave man some awesome power, the ability to create life, but that life came from a man and a woman and both is needed to mold that child into the person that God wants him to be.

Your beautiful gift from God is just floating in the atmosphere of life unclaimed by you. It is sad when someone is given a gift and they won't even accept it. Can you imagine how the giver feels, or how the gift itself feels? Have you ever been rejected? I have and it is a very painful thing, it affected my past, present, and future and made me feel less than, not quite good enough from childhood to adulthood. The only way I learned to love myself just the way I am and to accept the person that God made me to be is when I asked God to forgive me for not loving myself. You see God made me and I had some nerve telling God that I just wasn't good enough. Unfortunately, people, especially children, focus on the things they don't have and not on what they do have.

You see it is the devil that deceives people and makes them feel inferior. But when God made man He said these words "It is good." I want my grandson to always know that he truly is what God said he is, and so are you. Thank God for delivering me from the inferiority complex, and he will do the same for anyone that asks.

I want you to know that God loves you and has a special plan for your life, and He is just waiting for you to come to Him and receive it. It don't matter where you are or who you are, God wants to make things better for you, and most of all God wants to save your soul from the pits of hell to spend eternity in Heaven with Him.

I am praying that you will someday come and claim your gift (Nasir) from

God, but most of all I pray that you will claim your gift of eternal life through God's gift to the world, His Son, Jesus Christ.

Why don't you ask God to forgive you for your sins and to save your soul and make you the son and the daddy that He wants you to be?

Scriptures of love:

For God so loved the world, that He gave His only begotten Son, so that whosoever believeth in Him should not perish, but have everlasting life.

Roman 3:23–24 All have sinned and come short of the glory of God.

Roman 6:23 The wages of sin is death, but the gift of God is eternal life through Jesus Christ our Lord.

Roman 10:9–10 That if thou confess with thy mouth the Lord Jesus, and believe in thy heart that God hath raised Him from the dead, thou shall be saved. For with the heart man believeth unto righteousness and with the mouth confess unto salvation.

2 Corinthians 5:17 Therefore if any man be in Christ, he is a new creature: old things are passed away; behold, all things are become new.

Sincerely,

Bianca's mom, Beverly Allen

Beverly M. Allen


P.S. I asked Nasir if he could write his dad what would he say and this is what he said. He wrote this letter himself. His mom do not know about it.


    I love you

    Mommy loves you too

    -Nasir Allen Asante


Grandma Beverly lifts her hands, along with the hands of those in the circle beside her, and says, "Behold, I will heal thee. On the third day thou shalt go up unto the house of the Lord." Hands fall down in the amen circle.

The ER hum returns as I think about your powerful letter to your father; about the fathers, mothers, brothers, and sisters lost in Katrina. Lost because of their color, class, and/or creed.

**I was just a little girl caught up in the storm**
**And it still amaze me now I lived to see myself grown***

I think about how Katrina is still going, and not just in New Orleans, and I hear the words of Kim Rivers Roberts aka Black Kold Madina, "Katrina's not over. We still being affected right now. By not educating us, they're robbing out of the opportunity to be the next whoever. We got to go see how other people was living, it opened up our eyes. I mean it's like they preparing them for the future. Here in New Orleans, it's like they preparing us for prison. I'm here to represent the people who wasn't able to make it."

Kim is an amazing survivor and world-changing poet like you. Your sincere, raw, youthful message to your father penetrates my soul. Again, I think, look at the size of your heart, affirming to Uzi at just five that he is loved by you and your mother. Braveheart. You're a poet not because of the words you choose, but because your words and actions stand up amid the downpour. You are a poet because your words, back then and now, come from the same place that turned your slender body into a human shield to protect your little cousins from a storm of bullets.

---

* Black Kold Madina, "Amazing," *Trouble the Water*, 2008.

# 6 / Final Notice

Your letter arrives at Nna's apartment in Germantown. She's living on the twelfth floor of the Hathaway House, the building she calls "a big brown concrete monstrosity" on the corner of Chelten and Wissahickon.

Uzi is in and out of jail during the early 2000s like a revolving door. He gets arrested for riding a dirt bike on city streets (same thing Meek Mill got caught up for); having an open container of beer in public (hand-hugging a forty of Miller High Life outside the corner store); and probation violations.

> I'm *brap brap* Broad Street Yamaha Bikes
> That Stevie Williams, DGK, that grind life*

When your letter arrives in 2005, Uzi is not in jail. Nna calls him and says she has something to give to him (the letter from you and Grandma Beverly).

---

* Uzi, "Open Bar," *The Nephew Soundtrack*, 2024.

When he shows up to Nna's apartment, we embrace with electric, chaotic, excited energy. Every time I see him, it's been a *minute* and we both have deep love for each other. He's wearing a du-rag over cornrows that peak out the back, a Polo hoodie with the preppy teddy bear, gold grill fangs fixed across his front teeth, and a Newport loosie behind his ear.

**I'm on some other shit**
**I'm a 6'5 North-Face-Cuban-Link wearing Mothership***

"What's up, Mom?" he says, smiling at her in frosty 14K. Nna smiles back, basking in his presence, soaking in his powerful voice. She loves looking up at him and cheesing, marveling at his wit and beauty.

Uzi is the color of walnuts and has a long, sharp face like the African ceremonial masks fixed to the walls throughout Nna's house.

"This came for you sweetheart," she says, handing him the letter. He doesn't know what it is and he hesitates to grab it.

"What is it?"

"Read it!" Nna says, her pitch going higher. He takes it and she reaches up and rubs his face, shoulders.

"We'll give you some time to read it, sweetheart." Nna leads me out of the kitchen.

---

* Uzi, "Yachty Yada," *The Nephew Soundtrack*, 2024.

I sit with Nna in the living room while Uzi reads your letter in the kitchen. Nna's living room looks like a museum. African and African American art pieces stand boldly like soldiers in all directions. Eyes forward, chin up, at attention. Me and Uzi grow up surrounded by all of this art, all of these stories, colors, and voices.

On the mantle beside a classic picture of Uzi as a kid in an Izod sweater vest, there's a sculpture of a Chi Wara, the mythical antelope of the Bamana people from Mali. By the entryway is a life-size figure covered in cowrie shells—the world's first money—from the Bamileke of Cameroon. Above the entryway, a hammered aluminum piece by Olatunde called *Hunting in the Osogbo Forest*. A bronze hero on horseback from Benin sits atop the bookshelf along with pictures of Uzi, you, me, and Nna's dancers. On the wall there's a panel drawing by Richard Wyatt Jr. called *The Three Ages of Man* with drawings of a Black man as a boy, as a middle-aged man, and a white-haired old man. I think about you, Uzi, and your grandfather Bob.

On another wall hangs a pencil drawing called *Frustration* by Raymond Lark. *Frustration* shows a naked man on a bed with his head buried in his hands. He's surrounded by newspaper pages that read "Classified Ads" and papers that read "Final Notice." There's a Dogon statue of a man standing up, hands raised, representing the connection between heaven and earth.

> What's notable, I been winnin' awhile, I'm a dazzler
> Ancient astronaut from the Dogon Tribe, gangster tatted up*

---

* Dave East featuring Nas, "Godfather 4," *Survival*, 2019.

The biggest piece in the room is the mahogany Nimba statue from the Baga of Guinea. It's smooth and is of a woman with huge breasts, symbolizing fertility. A Senufo wooden drum, made by the Kulebele carvers, with scenes of lizards, horses, snakes, tortoises, and birds carved around it. Ceremonial masks from various ethnic groups—the Baluba, Bete, Dan, Ibibio, and Yoruba—hang high above it all.

Looking as regal as the historic Queen Nzinga of Ndongo and Matamba, Nna sits below a colorful framed painting of three kids dancing called *El Baile (The Dance)* by Elizabeth Catlett. A quote from the artist is printed underneath, reading: "Art must be realistic for me, whether sculpture or print making. I have always wanted my art to service black people."

Nna puts on a CD of one of her favorite artists, Miriam Makeba aka Mama Afrika! Afro-jazzy textures pour into us. I nod my head, vibing out. She says she discovered Miriam Makeba in the 1980s while we were all living in Zimbabwe.

**I shall sing, Sing my song**
**Be it right, Be it wrong***

"I absolutely love this music," she says, pearly and joyful, closing her eyes to remember pictures buried beneath braids. "She was our mother in struggle."

Nna moves to Zimbabwe in 1980, where I was born a year later. I'm born in Mbuya Nehanda Maternity Hospital in the capital city

---

* Miriam Makeba, "I Shall Sing," *Keep Me in Mind*, 1970.

of Harare, aka Sunshine City. "Mbuya" means "grandmother" in the Shona language and Nehanda is the traditional "lion spirit" that uses women to protect and fight oppression. The women around you—your mom, Nna, Grandma Beverly, Aunt Crystal—embody Nehanda.

At Lafayette College in Easton, PA, I'm fortunate to have a professor from Ghana, Dr. Kofi Opoku, who speaks in proverbs. Like, everything he says is a literal proverb, it's wild. He's an elder who owns and maintains an African Spiritual Technology forest called Anansekwae in the hills of Akuapem in Ghana. He's brimming with wisdom and lives in harmony with nature. I'm eternally grateful to his son, Nana Addo, my college roommate, for introducing me to the revolutionary music of Fela Kuti, Immortal Technique, Dead Prez, and J Dilla.

I think about something Dr. Opoku says—"Far is where mother is; where you will expend all effort, even to death, to get there."—as Nna tells me about the blood transfusion I received at birth.

"Zimbabwean blood saved your life, and don't you forget it," she likes to remind me, pointing at my face like a spot on the map and cracking up.

> **Realadelphia raised me crazy,**
> **Rocks in the system, 80s baby**
> **Mama knocked on wisdom, praise the lady,**
> **Shout out Zimbabwe, land that saved me***

---

* Ace Clark featuring MK Asante, "Runnin," *The Nephew Soundtrack*, 2024.

Nna, my dad, and Uzi move to southern Africa around the time Zimbabwe is being born as a country. The Second Chimurenga, a bloody guerilla war for liberation, is coming to an end. Bob Marley makes the song "Zimbabwe" in 1979, which instantly becomes the anthem for the Black freedom fighters, strapped deep in the bush with AK-47s and FN Mags, as they battle for their independence from England. "Music is the biggest gun, because it save not kill," is how Bob Marley once put it.

> So arm in arms, with arms,
> We'll fight this little struggle
> Cause that's the only way we can,
> Overcome our little trouble[*]

"Ladies and gentlemen, Bob Marley and the Wailers," is the first official sentence in Zimbabwe after the British Union flag of Rhodesia is lowered and the new flag of Zimbabwe—black, gold, red, and green with an African fish eagle—is raised high. Nna is in attendance April 18, 1980, at Rufaro Stadium as Marley performs "Zimbabwe"—the same song that fueled the revolution—at the country's historic independence ceremony.

A country being colonized is just like a person being enslaved. Think of the American Revolution, when America goes to war with Britain for its independence. "Give me liberty, or give

---

[*] Bob Marley, "Zimbabwe," 1979. While performing "Zimbabwe" during the independence ceremony, Marley was accidently teargassed by police. "Madness," Marley yelled as he ran off the stage. "And think, I have to come all the way to Africa to experience teargas."

me death!" New Hampshire's license plates say "Live Free
or Die." Same thing. In Zimbabwe, we go from Rhodesia, a
name honoring the racist genocidal maniac Cecil Rhodes, to
Zimbabwe, a Shona name that means "house of stones." It's
similar to how Nna changes her name from what she calls her
"slave name," Carole Ann, to Kariamu, a Swahili name meaning
"one who reflects the moon." My dad changes his name, too,
from Arthur Lee Smith to Molefi Kete Asante, Molefi meaning
"keeper of tradition," Kete meaning "royal drums," and Asante
meaning "thank you" in Swahili. They are also known as Amina
and Chaka in *Buck*.

Natty Dread it in-a (Zimbabwe)!
Set it up in (Zimbabwe)!
Mash it up-a in-a Zimbabwe (Zimbabwe)!
Africans a-liberate (Zimbabwe), yeah*

Nna becomes the first artistic director of the National Dance
Company of Zimbabwe. She choreographs dances to Miriam
Makeba and Nina Simone, as well as traditional Zimbabwean
music.

"My artistry draws from the calabash of African movement and
aesthetics," Nna says. "It's a deliberate choice that empowers me
to create new work that honors the traditions of those on whose
shoulders I stand." Nna's mention of "shoulders" sends me to
another Opoku proverb: "If we stand tall, it is because we stand on
the shoulders of our elders and ancestors."

---

* Bob Marley, "Zimbabwe," *Survival*, 1979.

Nna says that an artist is like a sponge.

"Myth, legend, and literature are all resources for me as are the sounds of Black people, the rhythms of the urban landscape, and the cavernous echoes of the rural South. Shona and Ndebele. Bed-Stuy. Nothing escapes my palette!"

"Brooklyn's finest!" I say, proudly celebrating her genius.

"Brooklyn, yes! Images of my mother singing in her bra and half-slip in the sticky humid August evenings in Brooklyn as she ironed, washed, and cleaned resonate with me not only as memory but also as movement, as narrative . . ."

When Nna moves back to America, she brings the sounds and music from Zimbabwe back with her. In her choreography, one of her staple pieces becomes "A luta continua" (the struggle continues) based on a Miriam Makeba song that, just like Marley's "Zimbabwe," is an anthem for the guerilla freedom fighters in Mozambique.

In Zimbabwe a luta continua
A luta continua, continua, continua*

Nna puts me and Uzi on to these powerful voices from the jump. We learn the power of Nommo, the concept of voice and sound to create harmony amid chaos. Remember I mentioned Randy Weston from Bed-Stuy? He discovers the same thing as Nna: "In Africa I

---

* Miriam Makeba, "A Luta Continua," *Welela*, 1989.

discovered what the true purpose of a musician is. We are historians, and it is our purpose to tell the people the true story of our past, and to extend a better vision of the future," says Weston before his death in 2018.

"Yo!" I hear Uzi in the other room.

Nna tries to get up from her burgundy sectional, but winces in discomfort.

"You go," she says in clear physical pain.

"Are you okay? Need anything mom?"

"I just need a minute." She grimaces. "Go talk to your brother." She smiles through the pain.

I join Uzi in the kitchen. He sits at Nna's favorite wooden table with your letter in front of him. His long six-five frame always strikes me like he plays in the NBA. He's tall even when he's sitting down, knees pointed to the sky. I place a gentle hand on the back of his hoodie as I sit next to him.

"So . . . ?" I say settling in to the strong, worn, woven leather chair. This is the same chair and table I've seen Nna reading her four newspapers a day at—*New York Times*, *New York Post*, *Philadelphia Inquirer*, and *Philadelphia Daily News*—plus her *New York Times* crossword puzzle.

**Game seven, Mama got the same tattered leather Bible**
**With rubbed off gold title, and the same reverend**

She put her unpaid bills in Psalms
And pray to God they get paid by the bank in Heaven*

"I don't know, man," he says after a while, shaking his head, staring at his size-fifteen Air Force 1s. I can see the weight on his spirit like the haze on a city skyline. I can feel the pressure on his soul like the death of a loved one. He takes a swig from the forty of Miller High Life tucked in a brown paper bag between his denim.

Even though he's not in jail when your letter arrives, I sense that he's already put up his own stone-cold prison walls. That he's erecting a self-made cell with no windows to let the light in. That he's acting as judge, warden, CO, and inmate in his own private Attica.

"It's never too late big bro," I remind him. "Never too late. No wrong time to do the right thing."

Uzi nods in agreement. This is a chorus Uzi knows well. We sing it to him from the moment you are born. We sing about the divine gift—you—that awaits his embrace.

Nna comes into the kitchen and we help her to sit down.

"You should know that you are brilliant," she tells Uzi, looking right at him.

He chuckles like he doesn't believe it.

---

* Uzi, "24 Hourz," *The Nephew Soundtrack*, 2024.

"And your son Nasir is brilliant. You must believe that," she reaffirms. "Your brother knows it." They look at me.

"Definitely," I say.

"Don't take time for granted," Nna warns. "None of us know how much time we have left on this planet. And sweetheart, you don't want to live a life full of regrets. Think about what happened with your father and his mom." This is the first time I ever hear Nna bring this up and I can see it immediately connects with Uzi. "Regret pain's heavy."

"You right, you right." He can't deny it. Nna kisses him all over his hands. "You were a labor of love, my firstborn. Talent is in you and all around us. Don't ever think that it is easy for any of us. We all have demons, sometimes skillfully tucked away in the deep pockets of our heart."

Uzi take it all in and finishes his beer. He laughs and jokes with us and tells stories about back in the days. He talks about Buffalo and upstate New York, going to Howard Johnson's with Nna. These memories make the room feel like the DeLorean time machine car with the butterfly doors in *Back to the Future*.

We dap each other up, hug, and I walk him to the door. We embrace and he jogs away down the dim hallway, fading away.

Watching him leave, I feel a sense of hope that he will reach out to you. I feel the sense that your letter just might be the wake-up call he needed to "Git up, git out, and git something" like that OutKast chorus.

When I get back to Nna's kitchen, reality hits me like a sucker punch. I feel like I got snuck by a mean one.

> **What the fuck do I tell them?**
> **If we the ones that trained them,**
> **Then we derailed them***

I can't believe it. Uzi leaves the letter on Nna's favorite table next to her *New York Times* crossword puzzle. How could he leave it? I think about Uzi jogging away and realize that he is running from himself—from his family, his talent, his gifts.

I think about the message of your letter and reflect on Grandma Beverly's question, "Imagine how the gift feels? The Giver?"

---

* Uzi, "24 Hourz," *The Nephew Soundtrack*, 2024.

# 7 / Double Dutch Chronicles

Later that night, Nna pulls her journal out. Her breathing is heavy and, for the first time, I notice that her hands are shaky. She spreads a colorful Faith Ringgold quilt over her legs and says that she's been in pain.

"Where?" I ask.

"Not in any one place, sweetheart, but everywhere." She smiles with her soft brown eyes, steady, shimmering, and as vast as galaxy marbles.

"Before I forget, what happened with Uzi's dad and his mom?"

Nna tells me that your grandfather Bob experienced a terrible tragedy as a teenager in Harlem, his hometown.

"His mom went to the market and told him to be downstairs when she got back to help her with the bags. She was older and they lived on the third floor of a building with no elevators and three steep flights of steps. She came back from the market, and for whatever reason, he wasn't there. As she carried the bags up the stairs by herself, she suffered a heart attack and collapsed down the stairs. By the time Bob got there, it was too late."

This is my first time hearing about this. I think about the fragility of life and how this one event affected generations. I think about my own mother, Nna, living on the twelfth floor of this "concrete monstrosity."

I kiss Nna on the forehead, then on the cheek. "I love you."

"I want to read something to you," she says, opening her journal, fixing her quilt.

"There's so much you don't know about your mother. I want you to know my story." I sink into Nna's couch, just like when I sink into the seats in the car, absorbing your story through the Meridian 13 speaker system. Nna reads to me and I feel the enchantment of a little kid at story time.

Dear Carole,

I remember running down the steps of my apartment building, although I didn't call it that then. It was summer and it seemed that everyone was outside. The stoops were crowded with mothers, sisters, grannies and Miss This and Miss That. But the people and the sounds that drew forth dimmed as I heard the magical sound of the girls chanting "ten, ten, ten, one ten, one twenty . . ." The ropes swung high in the air as Marcella swayed back and forth on her legs, drawing her arms back just so to position herself to propel into the rope with a little bobbing of the head, just enough to avoid hitting the rope. She was in! Then the dance began.

She steadied herself between the ropes, calculating the tones of the rhythms and if she should change her pace or steps. She was completely in the rhythm now, and it was time to turn and hop a little and turn some more, touch the ground and move to the left and then to the right.

Everyone watching was encouraging, and I stood where I always stood admiring Marcella but my yes riveted on the mechanics of the jumping and the soulful calls of the ropes. These were big girls jumping. They must have been ten or eleven. I was only six at the time and they didn't even think of me when they invited people to play.

Marcella jumped out with ease, never collapsing the ropes, which was a sign of a beginner. I was relegated to the single rope, and that was fine, but it was Double Dutch and its rhythms that were calling me! Ten, Ten, Ten, One Ten. Two Ten, Three Ten. Ya Bah Dee Da Bah Ya Ba De Ya Bah Yaaaaaah! What!

The various hues of brown, cocoa, almond, and cashew glistened in the sun. If they were sweating, I couldn't tell, instead I saw pearls running down their foreheads and necks. These girls were princesses, and I was their lady-in-waiting to enter that sacred arena and claim my place in the pantheon of jumpers.

One day they were short a jumper and they asked me. Didn't even know my name. Only knew I lived down the block. What! Me, jump, me, turn! At first, I turned to make sure, I wasn't doublehanded. That was when the turner would favor one side or the other and disrupt the evenness of the rope, making it more difficult for the jumper. I wound the ropes in each hand and I began to bob with the rhythms. I bent my knees, giving me freedom to move with the jumper not in competition with her, but as another element in the jumping game.

"Okay, little sis, it's your turn now. Do you want us to count you in?"

"No," I said. That's when someone couldn't jump into the rope and had to be helped. If you stood at the side trying to catch the rhythm too long, they would know you were a novice or scared of the rope and count you in anyway.

The ropes seemed huge. All of a sudden they seemed too big for a little girl like me.

But this was my chance.

"All, All, All in the Weather Girl, How you like the Weather Girl, Fine, Fine, Super Fine! Ten, Twenty" and I was in. I was jumping Double Dutch! I was dancing and the rhythms took me back and forward and back again.

I would never forget the intricacies of the ropes, and the more I played, the better I became. This was my first training. I could bob and weave with the best of them. I could go down and touch the ground and go up little buttercup. I could turn round and round and touch the ground. I could jump on one leg and then bring the second to mark the rhythm. I draw back my arms with my elbows flexed and my feet rocking back and forth in my "get ready" position to jump in the rope. One of the ropes had to be down in order for me to enter and I had to immediately shift my rhythm and gait so I would now jump without collapsing the ropes.

I expanded my repertory of moves. I could jump up and down with two feet and I could hop on one leg and turn around and then reverse it. I could go as fast as the turners could turn and they delighted in besting me and getting me out. I was now a part of what I considered the most important group in the world. I would complete chores as fast as possible so I could go outside and jump rope.

I was sought after and it thrilled me to hear "Carole is coming!" The streets of Brooklyn embraced me where all you needed was your mother's clothesline for a hot minute. What!

Twilight would come and the jumping would continue. We would exhaust their repertory of chants and songs. We even made up a few. The slowly darkening sky hovered above the girls as we jumped with energy, precision, and oblivion to the ensuing night and the calls of our mothers. I would have to be threatened to come inside. I could barely see the rope as it got darker but the rhythm guided me. Finally, after the second or third call from our mothers, we reluctantly turned in for the night.

Often we would engage in playing the dozens in the ropes. The fingers, hands, hips, and upper torso swayed to rhythms and beats that have already been spoken for and threw back what we could and walked away licking wounds when we couldn't throw down. We rehearsed the social performance of childhood and I learned something about this rite of passage, of coming into womanhood. The street was an arena of improvised gesticulations and time-honored rhythms from the recent and ancient past.

That was my training until little buds began popping up on my chest. They didn't move so much as they hurt. Although we had a way of dealing with the changes in our body. We would get in the rope and immediately cross our arms and put them over our chests. This not only minimized the breast bouncing, it kept the boys at bay. It goes without saying that the boys enjoyed watching the girls jump rope, but as they too grew into puberty, their focus began to shift. The final blow came when my menses started. My mother said "absolutely not." And that was the end of that! It was before tampons and such and I was so poor I would sometimes have rags in my panties that I would wash out every night. Double Dutch remained an activity, but girls were cautious especially around that time of the month.

Before I moved from Albany Avenue, beautiful tall buildings began to be built across the street. It was something that they called the projects. These new buildings represented "newness" and I longed for that experience. I wanted to know the feeling of five rooms and closets. I wanted to smell "clean!" I wanted to live in that city within the city. I had one experience in the "projects," and that solidified my desire to live in the "projects." The projects had an array of activities in their community center. One of the offerings was a dance class. I wrangled my way into the class even though these activities were only open to residents.

The class was a "modern" dance class and it was not memorable, but what was memorable was the beautiful African American teacher who taught the class. I was a creature from another world. I wanted to master this "modern" dance class, so the teacher would notice me. But this "modern" dance was a lot of stretching and bending. There wasn't any interesting music to move to, and in my mind, this wasn't dancing. Sad to say, after a few weeks, the teacher didn't come back and Albany Ave and the projects became a distant past, chanting with echoes of young girlhood and the awakenings of the new. New body, new apartment, maybe new friends and a new school—something to think about if not look forward to.

Gone were the summers filled with feet pumping up against pavements and shouts of encouragement. Gone was the attention and the satisfaction that I could do something right. Gone was the sight of two ropes crossing in the air, reaching for something that was unseen but definitely felt. I didn't know it but I would jump Double Dutch again. Never in the same way, but those three years of jumping would reward me tenfold as I entered womanhood.

The rhythms never left me. They were embedded in my spirit and soul. The steps were embodied and accessible, so that I could call on them in a moment's notice.

At our next apartment in Bushwick, I had new neighbors, heard new fights, saw one stabbing, and overheard curse words that I didn't know existed. The way those words jumped out of people's mouths. They could mow you down and leave you for dead. I had only heard my Mother say damn or (S)ugar, (H) oney, (I)ced, (T)ea., which I loved. Because if you said (S)ugar, (H)oney, (I)ced, (T)ea, you weren't really cursing. But these words had a power, an ability to raise voices, an ability to make men drunk with rage, and I saw grown women cry after being called "Black Ho." I liked listening to it even if it meant possible danger.

I met a new best friend, Eleanor. Eleanor lived in an apartment that ran the length of the entire floor and she had a mother and a father that lived together! She also had a TV. I was over there a lot. One day we decided to make up a dance. It was more like a pantomime, but that was not a term that we were familiar with yet. We moved to the song "It Took a Hundred Pounds of Clay." It was a popular song that was about God, I think. Eleanor's parents were delighted with our performance and Eleanor and I were quite pleased with ourselves. Years later, when I was a professional dancer, they came to see me dance.

In high school at Franklin K. Lane on the border of Brooklyn and Queens, a five-thousand-student gargantuan of a school that somehow was my own little private world, I was in the modern dance classes of Mrs. Ida Waranoff, a former Martha Graham teacher. She was a tiny woman, but she taught with strict rules and standards. These classes were in lieu of PE and one had to audition to get in. Well, I auditioned and I didn't get in. I first watched the modern dance club perform the previous year at a school assembly. I had never seen black girls dancing like this before. They were beautiful in a way that was completely new to me. This image was the motivation for me to audition for the club. The modern club was mostly white, but a few black girls did manage to get in. I was not one of them. What to do? I handwrote a letter from my mother saying:

Dear Mrs. Waranoff,

Thank you so much for taking the time to audition my daughter, Carole Welsh. She is devastated by the news that she didn't get into the modern dance club. This has been her dream since coming to FK Lane. If you could please reconsider or let her audition again, I would be most grateful. Thank you for your time and attention.

Thank you,

Ruth Hoover

Mrs. Waranoff called me into her office the following week and told me that I was accepted! The story doesn't quite end there. In class, I was the least formally trained but I loved the jumping and leaping sequences. In fact, one day, Mrs. Waranoff singled me out and said, "look at Carole, see how high she goes. What animal energy!" This was 1965 and this was the lay of the land. Her comments did not thwart my desire to "jump." There were auditions within the club to be in a dance that one of the members choreographed or Mrs. Waranoff choreographed.

When I wasn't selected for anyone's dance, including Mrs. Waranoff's, I went to her and asked her why wasn't I in anybody's dance?

She didn't have an answer for my question but she gave me advice that would change my life. She said, "the only way to make sure you are in a dance is to make it up yourself and put yourself in it!"

I had to wait until the following spring, but that is precisely what I did.

In my junior year in high school, I became aware of a jazz company called the Ron Davis Jazz Company. I think a flyer had been put up at my school announcing auditions. I knew next to nothing about jazz dance, or music for that matter, but I loved to dance. Ron Davis was the choreographer and artistic director. He had received a grant to take a group of dancers to four traditionally Black colleges in the South and expose them to jazz dance.

I was invited to be a part of that group of about 10 or 12 dancers. Ron's studio was in mid-Manhattan right near Broadway. It was on the second floor and we looked out at the streets of 8th and Broadway. Ron was interesting. He was a very thin man and wore classic black jazz pants and shoes with a black turtleneck. He was a chain-smoker and he said very little to us unless he was annoyed. I don't think I ever really saw him dance. He was able to convey to us what he wanted and we did it. I didn't have a clue about his background or what his credentials were, but there we were, mostly untrained dancers in his studio getting ready to tour the south. His repertory was great but favored the muscularity of the men, but the females had their moments and we relished them.

He introduced me to jazz artists like Jimmy Heath, and some others that I have to recall as well as Otis Redding's "Try a Little Tenderness," which bought the house down whenever we performed it in the south. We toured Virginia Union, South Carolina State, A&T in Greensboro, North Carolina, and Johnson C. Smith in Charlotte, North Carolina. We ran out of money and had to cut our trip short, or I should say that Ron ran out of money, which was a constant problem with him.

The trip was eventful. The changing of the landscape as we traveled south and crossed the Mason-Dixon Line was dramatic. Most of us were from poor neighborhoods and deteriorating apartment buildings, but we were looking at shacks and shotgun houses and somehow it didn't seem to be in the same category. Although we were teenagers we were all too aware that we were entering territory that could be dangerous to young black teenagers. I felt a sense of dread. If not for the moment, then the past. I could feel rhythms of people running and I heard heavy breathing, I was sure of it but when I looked around the bus, all I saw was sleeping teenagers.

This was 1966 and we were instructed about how we should talk to white folk and what we shouldn't do or say. We could feel the difference in the air, or so we thought, and although life on the campuses of these schools was more or less uneventful, there was a sigh of relief when we boarded the bus to take us back to NYC.

The jazz sounds of Ron's choreography bought new elements to my body. The pulse was still there, only now there were saxophones and bass holding the lines and I began to understand a little more about nuances and "dancing" the dance and letting the dance speak to me. Ya DA Ba Ba Da YA BABABADEEYABADEEYABADABADA!

This was a different echo from the streets and it landed right in my heart. I can still feel us dancing to this rhythm and little did we or Ron know it, we were a line of Nubian women, arms akimbo, thrusting our chests out and doing a neck dance. The southern landscape would reverberate with the cries of Emmett Till, the four little black girls killed in the Birmingham, Alabama, bombings, Medgar Evers, Viola Liuzzo, and John Chaney. Gulley after pond after ravine whispered to me as the bus sped down and up the highway, "We are here, waiting for you to hear our call and say your name." Somebody began to sing, "I am going up yonder." Instead of singing UP, he sang DOWN. We were indeed going down yonder. Each college seemed like the next. We performed in basketball arenas and football stadiums and acted like the sixteen and seventeen teenagers that we were. Several "hookups" were made during our brief tour and not a few southern fellows found themselves in the Big Apple looking for their loved one. What they didn't know was that these NYC dancers had nothing. All of us lived in cut-up tenements with no grass or trees in sight. They on the other hand lived in houses that they proudly owned on a nice piece of land, grew their own food, and their parents could help them go to what we now call an HBCU school. Funny thing, years later, I was traveling to Philadelphia when I saw Ron Davis in Grand Central Station and he was a homeless beggar. I recognized him immediately and wondered if I should go up to him. I didn't. It was sad. He ended up owing the dancers a lot of money, which he kept on saying that he was going to pay us but he never did.

I had another experience in high school that was interesting and almost prophetic. There was a West Indian girl in my class. We called them West Indians then just like I was a Negro. Her brother was having a party and she wanted me to dance with her at this party. She called it an African dance. I knew nothing about anything called an African dance. She taught me a dance and I loved it. She used music that I had never heard before, but it was rhythmic, pulsating, resonating, and propulsive. I melted into the music and the music found me, seeping into this Brooklyn teenager who wouldn't be able to find the West Indies or Africa on a map if my life depended on it. They were a huge success and little did I know that African Dance would embrace and rear me up into womanhood, into motherhood, into a profession and would save my life on not one, but several occasions.

In Buffalo while I was in college, there was no tradition of Double Dutch and so when spring came, a group of us from NYC arranged games in front of our dorm. The rhythms echoed from the sounds of the rope slapping the ground, our call and responses, and the sound of our feet striking the ground in intricate rhythms that went down into the earth and resounded back up in a chorus of cacophonic sounds and movements. Yah, Bah, Bah, Dee, Yaa, Ba, De, Ya, Ba, Ba, Baa Yaaah!

When I taught young girls at the YMCA, I searched for a way to reach these young girls who had never been exposed to any kind of dance except social dance. One day, when I was stretching with them, I started chanting and clapping. YAH, BAH, DEE, YAH, BAH, DEE, YAH, BAH, YAH, YAH, YAH! The energy in the class changed. Bodies perked up and I knew I had connected with them. I took it further. I began to do the Temptation Walk and they couldn't wait for me to stop demonstrating so that they could do it. I then took the Temptation Walk and closed the leg into a push-up so that the movement had a completely different feel. This was a growth process as well. This push-up would soon evolve into the samba and other variations of a 6/8 rhythm. I had connected with students in a space that we could both relate to. It was a joy to hear the class break out into a Temptations song as we did the walk!

Buffalo had its own rhythms and I often went into the "community" to experience some of "home." There were no tall projects, converted brownstones, or stoops where rhythms played out in a different mode. But there was the Fruit Belt, a neighborhood of small houses all clustered together with the world going by on their porches. The blues sauntered and sashayed out of those houses with the smell of fried chicken, macaroni and cheese, and cornbread to activate rhythms in all of their majesty.

My experience with the young women at the YMCA was the beginning of a dance technique that I would later call "Umfundalai." The rhythms from my youth were not only memorable, they were sustaining, translatable, and provided currency for me as I traveled the world. I taught dance at a community center in Lackawanna, NY, a steel town that sent out bellows of noxious odors as you drove into town. There, like so many places in America, there were many poor working-class Black people with children they longed to have a better life. I don't know if what I was offering was "better," but it echoed and resounded with rhythms they could relate to. I incorporated the never-ending sound of the steel mills that was a looming presence in their lives, a source of livelihood and a daily reminder of what it meant to be black in America.

I'm already embracing Nna as she closes her journal, my arms, neck, and head covering her like that colorful quilt on her lap. Nna is our sacred quiltmaker and listening to her inspires me. I think about how Nna's choreography and dance embody the quintessential elements of the Black freedom quilt.

The Black freedom quilt is the type of quilt that our people, mainly Black women, made for each other during slavery. These quilts were extraordinary and sacred for four reasons.

The first is that they illustrated our resourcefulness. Due to our status as enslaved, we had access to only scrap material. However, with scraps, we made something out of nothing, spun gold from wax, and maximized minimal resources. When Nna talks about using the rhythms from Brooklyn double Dutch or the whirring from upstate New York steel mills to make choreography, she is dancing in the tradition of the Black freedom quilt.

The second element of the Black freedom quilt is that despite having limited resources, they were exceptionally beautiful. They hold up today as aesthetic marvels of vivid color and imagination. Nna's choreography, despite any personal setback or struggle, is always up to the highest aesthetic standards. The beauty of her choreography dances in the tradition of the Black freedom quilt.

The third element that jumps out at me about our ancestor's quilts is that they were not just resourceful, but also practical. Although the quilt is a piece of art, its intent is functional and practical. The poet Amiri Baraka once said that art "is something the West has never understood. Art is supposed to be a part of a community. Like, scholars are supposed to be a part of a community . . . Art is to decorate people's houses, their skin, their clothes, to make them expand their minds, and it's supposed to be right in the community, where they can have it when they want it . . . It's supposed to be as essential as a grocery store . . . that's the only way art can function naturally." When Nna talks about putting on dance performances for free on stages in the hood or teaching in the YMCA, she's dancing in the folds of the Black freedom quilt.

One of Nna's dance students, Joselli, once explained that, "Mama Kariamu teaches our dancing bodies and our dancing minds. She grounded us in our epic memories, and the movement and philosophies of our ancestors, so that we can connect to them and find the best expressions of ourselves. We then plunge boldly into our futures empowered and enabled. We find our voices. Hers is not an elitist, exclusive invitation to learn and be nurtured, but it involves everyone, no matter what age, race, gender, sexual orientation, or life situation. One of the most essential things that I learned from Mama Kariamu is that 'no one should be left behind.'"

> I cannot forget my ancestors just because I rap, rap, rap
> Look at me from top to bottom, KRS is Black, Black, Black*

The last element of the Black freedom quilt is mind-blowing. Our ancestors, while enslaved, would encode symbolic messages on the quilts, just like they did with the songs. Sometimes they were maps, information about safe houses, and other codes that would aid runaways. For instance, the patterns "wagon wheel," "tumbling blocks," and "bear's paw" all contained secret messages that helped

---

* KRS-One, "Black Black Black," *Between da Protests*, 2020.

the enslaved navigate the Underground Railroad. One of the Underground Railroad safe houses, the Johnson House, is just a few blocks from Nna's apartment in Germantown. When Nna tells us about her work in Zimbabwe, working with warring tribes, uniting them through movement, she is dancing in the tradition of the Black freedom quilt.

The quilts our ancestors made, while enslaved, were resourceful, beautiful, useful, and emancipatory. Nna dances in that same rich tradition of Black art and just like double Dutch, Nephew, it is your turn.

# 8 / The More Things Change

When Uzi finally answers the phone, he tells me that he left the letter by "mistake" and will come back to get it.

"My bad," he says nonchalantly like he dialed the wrong number.

He never comes back. Days become months and months become closing storm windows. His neglect eats at me daily, violently like cancer.

His response, or lack of response, changes the dynamics of our brotherhood. It's like a 180-degree flip. Growing up, he's a hero of a big brother and I follow him like a bot. I can remember, as a young buck, trying to roll with my big bro:

*This is how it always goes: me following Uzi in everything, everywhere, like his little black JanSport, covered in Marks-A-Lot, strapped tight to his back—Koala-style. Anywhere, anyplace. He does it, I do it. He tries it, fuck it, I'm trying it. He can, shit, why can't I? Sometimes I even duck like him under doorways, even though he's way taller and I don't need to duck. I don't care that he's taller, or older, or smarter.*

I feel my childhood idol idling in childhood and it's devastating. I recognize that back when we were kids and I idolized him, we didn't have any responsibilities. As easy as it is for me to idolize him back then, it's painful to see him self-destruct now. How does my towering big bro dwarf into a lost little bro?

I hit his phone every chance I get. His answers are few and far between, but when he responds, I continue to voice my concern.

"You can't win, at anything, if you turn your back on your kid," I warn him on the horn. The deadbeat path is a spiritual dead end that I urge him to reverse course on. "C'mon big bro, it's not too late."

**Blame yourself if I said I don't never need you**
**First tried to reach out to you but ain't never reach you***

As the silence from your dad intensifies, my voice as an uncle— "Unc," as you call me—amplifies. I commit myself to being the best unc I can be. I realize that I can't control what kind of father Uzi is, but I can control what kind of uncle I am. Opoku always says "it takes a village to raise a child." This is part of our African roots.

Opoku says, "Even in a foreign habitat, a snail never loses its shell." I see this for myself when I travel to Africa—Ghana, Senegal, Zambia, Namibia, Nigeria, Uganda, Zimbabwe, South Africa, Lesotho, Mozambique—and see Black people moving to the same beat as they do in North Philly or Compton. Through my travels in over twenty African countries, I also learn that the uncle in many

---

* Neph, "Glad at You," *The Nephew Soundtrack*, 2024.

cultures serves an essential role in the fam. In Setswana, the uncle is called *malome*, which means the "one who puts things together." In West Africa, when there's a conflict, the uncle is called to resolve or mediate; when there's a wedding, it can't begin until unc arrives; and the brother of a deceased man is called father by the late brother's children.

**Dear nephews, I'm writing this with no pen or a pad**
**And I'm signing it, your uncle, your best friend, and your dad***

Even the rap name that you choose for yourself—"Neph"—is a powerful testament to your identity and history. Names define us, speak to our collective past and our tomorrow. Names aren't just about what they call you, but what you answer to, and even more, what you call yourself.

**Dear sister, got me twisted up in prison, I miss ya**
**Cryin', lookin' at my nieces and my nephew picture†**

As African-Americans, we retain many elements of African culture. In addition, hundreds of years of enslavement split up the Black family unit—with family members being auctioned to enslavers throughout America—so it's no wonder why we have strong extended familial ties. Notice how in Philly we all say "fam" to people who aren't our actual family members. *What's up fam?* The OG's even say "family." *You good, family?* Or how your friend is the

---

* Jay-Z, "Anything," *Vol. 3 . . . Life and Times of S. Carter*, 1999.
† Tupac Shakur, "White Manz World," *The Don Killuminati: The 7 Day Theory*, 1996.

"bro" or "sis." How everybody is everybody's "cousin." I remember when I first met my mentor, Dr. Maya Angelou. I go to her beautiful sunny yellow house in Winston-Salem, North Carolina.

When I say, "Good morning, Dr. Angelou," she corrects me.

"It's Auntie Maya," she says with warmth, authority, and grace.

This is the "village" it takes. Of course, you experience this village all of the time. Every old head that you run into in Philly is going to automatically call you "Nephew" because that's our culture—family. And the same for you, your default is to call an old head "unc."

Auntie Maya Angelou sends me a letter shortly after I sent her a copy of my first memoir, *Buck*. Uzi's letter from prison and Auntie Maya's letter are the two most important and cherished letters I have ever received. She didn't just tell me to call her "Auntie," she guided and mentored me like kin. When I finish writing my memoir *Buck*, before anyone else reads it, I send it to her.

Auntie Maya responds with a beautiful letter. She tells me that when she first saw the title, *Buck*, she was reminded of a racist advertisement she saw as a child "praising the power of linens sold by one of America's powerful cotton mills." She explains that the ad showed an exhausted Native American man and woman with a crumpled dollar bill and "informs the viewer that this is an image of a Buck well spent." I think about all of the meanings of buck— young buck, buck wild, buckshots, Bucktown, Black buck, slave buck, make bucks, buck now.

Auntie Maya says that as she read my memoir, read about our family and our city, she realized that "the more things change, the more they remain the same." She acknowledges the progress that has been made, but reminds me that "our work remains to be done."

Auntie Maya tells me that *Buck* is a "story of surviving and thriving with passion, compassion, wit, and style." She finishes the letter with the most encouraging words I've ever received: "Yes, MK Asante, please continue to live, to accept your liberation, to accept how valuable you are to your country and admit that you are very necessary to us all."

Before I ever became a dad—to Aion, Wonderful, Nova, Akira and Akila, or became a youth basketball and soccer coach, or joined the PTA—I was your uncle first. You are about a dozen years older than my firstborn. As your uncle, I learn valuable lessons about responsibility and sacrifice, both building blocks on the road to becoming "Baba," the Swahili term for father.

**Girl dad, rest in peace to Kobe Bryant**
**When we teachin' our babies, we teach 'em heavy science***

I reflect on my own father, who many people around the world call Baba. Through his life and actions, my dad built a beautiful baba blueprint to follow. My father's influence on me as a father, uncle, and man illuminates my path with you.

"As his uncle, you are a father figure," he tells me, back in the day, about you. My dad is one out of sixteen children so he's been an uncle most of his life. He says, "You must teach him character

---

* Papoose featuring Saigon, "Heavy Science," *July*, 2021.

and integrity. Expose him to the world. Show him black excellence and love."

As a kid, my dad exposes Uzi and me to Afrocentricity. I remember:

*The newspapers call our father "the father of Afrocentricity" because he created it.*

**My third eye is my rail, on this L of thought**
**With Afrocentric stamps I'm mailing thoughts***

*Pops is always preaching Afrocentricity. He was a Church of Christ minister way back when, one of those child preachers, and he still sounds like he's in the pulpit when he talks about Black people, white people, and the struggle. I remember this debate he took me to at East Stroudsburg University a few years back: him vs. Cornel West vs. Arthur Schlesinger. It was packed, standing room only. I remember how West, this cool Black dude with a big Afro and a tight three-piece suit, talked with his hands flying fast like he was conducting an orchestra. And how Schlesinger, this old white guy with hair the color of milk and a red bow tie, sounded like a statue. I remember the cheers, the boos, the ad-libs. Most of all, though, I remember how dope my pops was: his passion, energy, confidence, intelligence. Half the time I didn't even know what he was talking about—hegemony . . . pedagogy . . . subverting the dominant paradigm—but I was proud.*

In the mid-2000s, I jet around the city with you like my copilot on some Wilbur and Orville Wright in Kill Devil Hills–type time.

---

\* Common, "All Night Long," *One Day It'll All Make Sense*, 1996.

I take you everywhere with me—on a Black boy joyride—and it reminds me of how I used to follow your dad around the city, a decade earlier, when I was a young buck in the nineties.

*I follow Uzi to sweaty Badlands house parties that always end in crazy, shirtless rumbles with everybody howling "Norf-side! Norf-side!" in the middle of the street. To Broad and Rockland to cop dime bags from one of the dusty bodegas with nothing but baking soda and expired Bisquick on the shelves. To freestyle ciphers on South Street that the nut-ass police always break up for no reason. To crack on jawns getting off the El at Sixty-Ninth street, like, "Yo, shawty, let me holla at you for a minute." To scale the fence to watch Sad Eye, the Jordan of street ball, hoop at Sixteenth and Susquehanna. To skate the ledges and steps at Love Park until we get chased away by the cops. To bomb the Orange Line subway with Sharpies and Kiwi polish sticks.*

We go to the Wachovia Center in South Philly to watch the Sixers hoop. You stand on top of your seat from the nosebleed section, cheering as Iverson crosses-up defenders. We jog under the flags of the world downtown along Museum Mile on our way to the Franklin Institute to eat Astronaut freeze-dried ice cream from the gift shop and watch that classic IMAX *Philadelphia Anthem* intro. The intro—the flashes of every part of the city, all the cultures and flavors—always makes me proud of Philly. After the museum, we grab cheesesteaks from Max's on Erie Avenue or go uptown for a fish platter from Garden of Bilal on Wadsworth Avenue.

Driving around with you in the car, I put you on to neo soul music from Philly artists like Jill Scott, Bilal, and Musiq Soulchild. I look over at you and quiz:

"Nephew, what we listening to?"

"Soullll music," you say with all your little kid teeth.

"Preach!"

As a young buck I remember my dad driving me around Philly to hit up various places. He didn't play much music in his car, but tapes of speeches from Black leaders like Marcus Garvey, Malcolm X, and John Henrik Clarke. For pops, every moment—a quick trip to the store, a ride to school—is a teaching moment. One of his go-to tracks in the car is a speech by Philly born-and-raised pastor Jeremiah Wright. The speech is called "What Makes You So Strong, Black Man?" and now, as I think about your strength nephew, I remember the crackly cassette:

> *"What makes you so strong, Black man? How is it that three hundred and seventy years of slavery, segregation, racism, Jim Crow laws, and second-class citizenship cannot wipe out the memory of Imhotep, Aesop, Akhenaton, and Thutmose II? What makes you so strong, Black man? . . . How is it that after all this country has done to you, you can still produce a Paul Robeson, a Thurgood Marshall, a Malcolm X, a Martin King, and a Ron McNair? What makes you so strong, Black man? . . . This country has tried castration and lynching, miseducation and brainwashing. They have taught you to hate yourself and to look at yourself through the awfully tainted eyeglasses of white Eurocentric lies, and yet you keep breaking out of the prisons they put you in. You break out in a W. E. B. Du Bois and a Booker T. Washington.*

I don't play speeches in my car, but a lot of albums that we listen to have interludes of speeches or interviews or movie clips.

I turn them up like a beat. On *Mos Def & Talib Kweli Are Black Star*, there's a clip from the movie *The Spook Who Sat By the Door*: "I was BORN Black, I -LIVE- Black, and I'm gonna die, prob'ly -BECAUSE- I'm Black, because some Cracker that -KNOWS- I'm Black, better than -YOU-, Nigga, is prob'ly gonna put a BULLET in the back of my head!" Dead Prez's album, *Let's Get Free*, uses the intro from Omali Yeshitela:

> *I'm not a hunter but I am told*
> *That in places like in the Arctic*
> *Where indigenous people sometimes might hunt a wolf*
> *They'll take a double edged blade;*
> *And they'll put blood on the blade*
> *And they'll melt the ice and stick the handle in the ice*
> *So that only the blade is protruding*
> *And that a wolf will smell the blood and want to eat*
> *And I'll come and lick the blade, trying to eat*
> *And what happens is when the wolf licks the blade*
> *Of course, he cuts his tongue, and he bleeds*
> *And he thinks he's really having a good meal*
> *And he drinks, and he licks, and he licks*
> *And of course, he is drinking his own blood and he kills himself*
> *That's what the Imperialists did to us with crack cocaine*
> *You got these young brothers out there thinking that they're getting*
> *something that they're gonna make a living with . . .*
> *And they actually think that there's something that's bringing*
> *resources to them*
> *But they're killing themselves just like the wolf was licking the blade*
> *And they're slowly dying without knowing it*
> *That's what's happening to the community, you with me on that?*
> *That's exactly and precisely what happens to the community*

*And instead of blaming the hunter who put the damn*
*Handle and the blade in the ice for the wolf*
*What happens is the wolf gets blamed for trying to live*
*That's what happens in our community*
*You don't blame the person, the victim*
*You blame the oppressor!*
*Imperialism, white power is the enemy*
*Was the enemy when it first came to Africa*
*Snatched up the first African;*
*Brought us here against our will*
*Is the enemy today*
*That's the thing that we have to understand*

With Dead Prez and Black Star bumping in the background, I take you with me any chance I get. I bring you to my book signing for my poetry book *Beautiful. And Ugly Too* at the African American Museum in Philly when you are seven. I bring you to Cinemark in University Center for the movie premiere of *The Black Candle*, my directorial debut narrated by Maya Angelou, when you are nine. At six years old, you star in my first short film made by Broad Street Productions. We ride down Frankford Avenue in Kensington—with no film permits whatsoever—in an old beat-up Benz with a camera jimmy-rigged to the front, filming you through the windshield. You're in the front seat, playing the role of a kid, next to the actor Khalil Munir, who drives the whip.

After the shoot, we hit up the Jamaican Jerk Hut on South Street and you fall in love with Caribbean food: roti, curry, brown stew snapper, plantains, patties, cocoa bread, and fried dumplings.

Motion is perpetual, street but intellectual
Anybody can get it, the work omni-directional
Stick with the auto-switch, semi-professional
Brown stew snapper rice & peas with the vegetables*

I introduce you to my tribe of friends in the village. I teach you to look everyone in the eyes, stand strong, and always stay on point. You take a liking to one of my best friends, who I call my brother—Dustin Felder, aka "Big Dus." Dustin is big in every way; his husky six-six NFL linebacker frame, his commanding James Earl Jones–type voice, his heavy laugh, the moves he makes, and his impact on me.

Big Dus gets hype when he sees us.

"M-Keezy" is what he calls me. "Nephew!" is what he calls you. Dustin is a professional actor and has been acting since he was a kid—Coke commercials, *Law & Order*, *New York Undercover*, the list goes on. Dustin moves to LA when he's like eighteen. Using that Philly-bred ambition, focus, and relentless hustle, he becomes one of the top acting coaches in Hollywood, and his films have made more than $1.7 billion in the box office.

On your eleventh birthday I take you to see Dustin's film *The Karate Kid*, about a twelve-year-old kid from Detroit who moves to China after his dad dies. You love the film, especially the fight sequences, and connect with Jaden Smith's character. Will Smith is a mentor to Dustin, and Dustin is the acting coach for Jaden

---

* MK Asante, "Brown Stew Snapper," *The Nephew Soundtrack*, 2024.

in *The Karate Kid*, *Pursuit of Happyness*, and *After Earth*. He also coaches Will and Jada's daughter, Willow, in the movie *I Am Legend*.

Dustin comes back to Philly a few times a year to see his folks and teach exclusive classes for actors in the Philly area. I take you to sit in on his master class. The class is packed with people from all backgrounds and walks of life. You're a young buck, but you watch the class intently.

"I call this the rubber band method," he says to the class, holding up a rubber band. He puts the rubber band on a table.

"What good is this rubber band in this position?"

"No good," someone throws out.

"Useless! It's useless. But watch . . ." Dustin says as he grabs a screenplay on the table. He stretches the rubber band around the pages, holding them together.

"Now it's stretching, keeping the pages together, fulfilling its purpose. We are the rubber bands, y'all. Dig me? We are the rubber bands. If you're not stretching yourself, as an actor, as a person, then you are not living your purpose. Acting is about stretching, not to your breaking point, but to your purpose point. Stretch yourself into purpose."

His class is philosophical and inspires excellence. Dustin is the same way in high school. He's one of the reasons I get my shit together. Since high school, when we met at Crefeld, the same school I send you to, he's held me to a high standard. He's always believed in me, even when I didn't believe in myself.

Dustin is from North Philly, Twentieth and Lehigh, two blocks from where you were born and raised, and three blocks from where you were shot. I introduce you to him to show you what's possible, who's accessible, and to put you up on game.

In my life, mentors have played an important role. Life is a journey and mentors are path lights perfectly positioned to illuminate our way along the stony roads we trod.

You love the neo soul music I play in the car, but one day, when you're about eleven, you say you want to hear rap. I'm like, *That's what's up.* Most of the rappers you want to hear are actually from your neighborhood: State Property, Oschino, Young Chris, and Freeway. Beanie Sigel is from South Phil, but you rock with him, too.

"Beans," you say, nodding your little head. You always want that real rap, even back then, so that's probably why you spit that realness now.

> It's about time we have a father to son
> Sit down let me tell you 'bout your fatherless sons*

One winter, we listen to Beans's heavy verse on Jay-Z's "Where Have You Been" as we drive through a snowy, uptown Philly. Icicles

---

* Jay-Z featuring Beanie Sigel, "Where Have You Been," *The Dynasty: Roc La Familia,* 2000.

like crystal chandeliers point down from corner store awnings.
Entrepreneurs with shovels and hustle clearing snow-covered
driveways and parking pads.

**We never kicked it at all,**
**We never pitched or kicked at a ball***

This is the song where Beans and Jay talk about their absent
fathers and the effect it had on their lives. I look over and I see real
tears building in your eyes—they run when you blink.

**You left us with no letters, notes, no replies (Nothing!)**
**No digits, numbers was unlisted**
**You left us with some of my loneliest nights**
**Ngh, some of my hungriest nights†**

The first song I ever cry to is Sam Cooke's "A Change Is
Gonna Come." It happens not too long ago, I'm driving down
Greenmount Avenue in Baltimore, which is like Lehigh Avenue in
Philly, listening to the French horns blare. I hear the song all my
life. I remember crying to it when Nna took me to see the movie
*Malcolm X*. Spike Lee uses the song as Malcolm—who says he isn't
afraid to die because "I live like a man who is dead already"—is
preparing for his last speech at the Audubon Ballroom in Harlem.
The song comes on in a shuffle mix and, because I haven't
seen Uzi in so long, I just lose it when Sam riffs on about his
brother . . .

---

*† Jay-Z featuring Beanie Sigel, "Where Have You Been," *The Dynasty: Roc La
Familia*, 2000.

> Then, I go to my brother
> And I say, "Brother, help me, please"
> But he winds up knockin' me
> Back down on my knees, oh*

For our tears, Beanie Sigel and Sam Cooke are the triggermen. Shortly after listening to that song, you tell me that you want to rap. You want to do for others what listening to Beans does for you.

It's powerful when art can invoke that kind of emotion in us. James Baldwin—the author of *A Fire Next Time*, which contains "My Dungeon Shook: Letter to my Nephew on the One Hundredth Anniversary of the Emancipation"—once said, "You think your pain and your heartbreak are unprecedented in the history of the world, but then you read . . ." Yes, you read Assata Shakur or Sister Souljah or NoViolet or Aja Monet. . . Or you listen to *The Reason* or *The Miseducation of Lauryn Hill or good kid, m.A.A.d City* . . . or you see *Sankofa* or *Pumzi* or *Moonlight* . . . or hear Sunni Patterson, Coast Contra, Uzi, or Neph. Yeah, you Neph. You write lifelines the same way Beans "paints pictures on the canvas of life."

Your birth ushers in new waves of thought for me. I think about what it means to be a man, about honor, about the building and maintaining of character. Opoku says, "great sailors aren't made on smooth seas." I think about my professor's words and how Uzi is navigating these choppy waters. And look at you, nephew,

---

\* Sam Cooke, "A Change Gonna Come," *Ain't That Good News*, 1964.

rowing upstream, pushing through the storm with courage and determination.

> I guess I love a lot, because the more
> I do my thang, the more I feel the guilt and shame that my brother's not*

The more time I spend with you, the harder it is for me to see Uzi. My love for Uzi is immense, but it's hard to reconcile his neglect.

The irony is that Uzi is the one that introduces me to the elements of hip-hop—graffiti, MCing, breakdancing, and DJing. I remember when I was four, he teaches me to breakdance in my burnt brown penny loafers at the Philadelphian. Coming up, Uzi's room is like a record store with *Word Up* magazine posters everywhere: Kool G Rap, EPMD, Big Daddy Kane, the Fat Boys, Rob Base, Eric B and Rakim, Cool C, NWA, the Ultramagnetic MC's, Crown Rulers, PE, and DJ Jazzy Jeff & the Fresh Prince.

> It's new. It's out of the ordinary
> It's rather extraordinary, so yo bust this commentary
> A literary genius and a superior beat creator†

Later in life, another MC, Labtekwon from Baltimore, schools me onto the fifth element of hip-hop: knowledge, wisdom, and understanding. This element is the hydroelectricity that is meant to flow through our bars, tags, breaks, and turntables.

---

\* Cozz featuring J. Cole, "Knock tha Hustle (Remix)", *Cozz & Effect*, 2014.
† DJ Jazzy Jeff & the Fresh Prince, "Brand New Funk," *He's the DJ, I'm the Rapper*, 1988.

The clock becomes a timebomb. Uzi's silence is louder than the music we love. It gets one hundred times harder to reconcile when I become a father myself. It becomes unimaginable.

Nna's like, "I don't even mention Nasir to Daudi when I talk to him once in a blue moon. What is the point? He knows that he has a child and if he doesn't want to acknowledge it, that is on him."

Then one day—boom!—*it* hits me like a hard foul: Uzi's absence is part of a continuum, like an "and one" continuation foul in basketball. He's doing what his dad did to his "gift" and what you must never do to your "gift."

# 9 / Mayor of the Ghetto

I didn't get a chance to meet Uzi's dad, your grandfather Bob, but as a kid, I hear about him all the time like an urban legend. Uzi raves about him, singing a hero's song about his dad whom he affectionately calls "pops." I remember him singing about how "Bob runs shit in Harlem, from one-two-fifth to the Heights; how he is the GOAT on the basketball court; how everybody calls him the mayor of the ghetto; how he's always rocking the fly shit before everyone else—fitteds, jerseys, fedoras; how he curses up a storm, all types of fucks and shits and bitches—hurricane slang."

Growing up, Uzi's song is the only tune I know about Bob until this one night, when Uzi's not home, and my mom sings the remix. The remix says that Bob is indeed brilliant, but that's he's all strung out on heroin; that he beats her like Ike Turner did Tina; and that my mom's neighbor, a priest, pulls a gun on Bob and tells him if he ever touches her again, he'll be "summoned to appear before his maker." This is the remix that spills out.

Around the same time I hear this remix, Uzi is getting into trouble at different schools in Philly, so Nna sends him to the

Piney Woods Country Life School, a historically Black boarding school in Mississippi. The TV show *60 Minutes* does a special on the school, saying, "The kids come to Piney Woods because they, or their parents, or someone in the neighborhood wanted to save them. Every one of them faced hopelessness at home, at school, or at both."

Nna's bandwidth to save Uzi is boundless. Your dad struggles in school from an early age. Not academically—bro is a certified genius—but behaviorally. The acting out starts early for Uzi. In 1981, when Uzi is seven and I'm not even born yet, his elementary school teacher writes a desperate letter to Nna.

Dear Kariamu,

Your son is having severe problems and causing them in the classroom for other students. He does not appear to be in control of himself. Perhaps it is the diet or possibly lead content. Whatever it is, in spite of his stated desire to "be good," it seems he is completely unable to control his behavior.

He has been very irritated as of late. He can put up with no frustration, and hits people quite frequently. Every day, students in my own class and others complain to me about his actions. I know he is quick to respond when he feels aggression, but many of the children complaining are only innocent bystanders when his breaking point is reached.

Your son is displacing his problems on others. Says others "make" him do things. He accuses me often of treating him badly and not liking him because he is Black. This is a bad attitude to develop as he will always be Black, and in all likelihood, will have to deal all his life with white people.

He is a kind, loving child. He possesses a tremendous leadership potential. He is creative, intelligent, and original. He has a sense of humor and a strong desire to please. Unfortunately he does not seem to be able to function in a large group for educational purposes.

The situation, as it stands, is not beneficial to him and is detrimental to the rest of the class. He seems to have the potential, as I stated before, but is apparently unable to capitalize on it.

I have hesitated to tell you of specific instances of poor behavior. For one reason, he truly seemed to want to improve. For another, his behavior is consistently disruptive and antiproductive. I wanted to avoid the "grocery list" of wrongdoings. "Hit people 4 times, spit twice, tapped his hands continually during reading and math, refused requests of teachers 6 times, had to be removed from class 4 times, etc., etc., etc."

His growth from September to December was considerable. Since January, however, the classroom has been intolerable due to his influence.

It is important that we meet soon to determine what is best for him.

Now fast-forward back to Piney Woods, a school that was founded to educate the illiterate children of formerly enslaved Africans. It's a no-nonsense, deep-South, Black-excellence boarding school in what Uzi calls "East Bumblefuck, Mississippi." Uzi says the principal is just like Mr. Clark from the movie *Lean on Me*.

"Discipline is not the enemy of enthusiasm," Uzi says, holding an imaginary bullhorn, doing his best Morgan-Freeman-as-Mr.-Clark impression. "Look at me, boy! Don't you smoke crack?" Uzi's hilarious.

This kind of school resonates with my dad, Uzi's stepdad, who is from the South. Born in 1942 in Valdosta, Georgia, on the banks of the Okefenokee Swamp and Withlacoochee River, he's the oldest boy of sixteen kids. He spends his early years picking cotton and working the fields. He's a no-nonsense type just like the principal at Piney Woods or Mr. Clark.

Carved in stone around the school are the phrases "Success Depends Upon Yourself" and the Latin phrase "Labor Omnia Vincit," which means "Work Conquers All."

Uzi's at Piney Woods for about a good month before Nna gets the dreaded call one night. I ear-hustle bits and pieces: Uzi gets caught in the girls' dorm . . . then gets into a fight with some guy from New York . . . breaks dude's nose. They send him back home to Philly with the quickness.

"I want to be with my real pops," Uzi declares when he gets back to Philly.

He asks our parents if he can go live with his dad, Bob, back in Buffalo. They say yes and Uzi jump-steps from Mississippi to Philly to Buffalo in the same year.

**I know heartbreak, I know betrayal**
**Walk by the mirror cause I don't want to see you fail**\*

I don't know exactly how it went down in Buffalo or why, just that *it* went down. He's only in Buffalo for a few weeks before my mom gets a call from Bob, angry, yelling at the top of his lungs.

"If you don't come get this boy . . . I'm-a kill him!"

Uzi never tells me what happens up there in Buffalo. The story I hear is that they get into a big, knock-down, drag-em-out fight on

---

\* Uzi, "24 Hourz," *The Nephew Soundtrack*, 2024.

the basketball court. They're both tall, competitive, rhythmic, and love basketball. But cymbals clash. Uzi's hero song fades out.

And this is the last time Uzi ever sees his pops . . . ever.

What could make a man do that do his son? What squabble over b-ball could lead to a dead silence? What happened to Bob?

My heart hurts for young Uzi.

# 10 / Astronaut Man

Bob starts his series of letters to God in the summer of 1971, three years before Uzi's born, right as NASA's Apollo 15 is landing on the moon. Uzi actually has a song about heroin called "NASA" which is super heavy—*my Uzi weighs a ton*—because that's the monkey that clings to Bob's back like a jet pack. The connection that Uzi, through his lyrics, and Bob, through his letters, share is powerful and profound. They speak to each other behind walls and bars, across generations, father and son, worlds apart but in the same cell.

> **I'm an Astronaut Man and I'm bout to go outta space**
> **But on some real shit I'm just trying get the fuck up out this place**
> **Lost my spirit and my soul so I'm just trapped without a faith**
> **and I can't stop running cause my head is in constant chase**\*

The Vietnam War rages in the summer of '71. The Champ, Muhammad Ali, is on TV asking, "Why should they ask me to put on a uniform and go ten thousand miles from home and drop bombs and

---

\*   Uzi, "NASA," *The Nephew Soundtrack*, 2024.

bullets on Brown people in Vietnam while so-called Negro people in Louisville are treated like dogs and denied simple human rights?"

Like Uzi, your grandfather Bob was a gifted writer. He documented his violent personal war in his battered brown journal with the words "Me, Myself and I—The Thoughts of Robert Allen Jackson" written on the front in navy ink. His handwriting, just like graffiti-writing Uzi's, is a unique, masterful, fluid script that reminds me of Arabic calligraphy. Smooth, strong, and wavy like Van Gogh granite.

Bob's journal has two inscriptions written on the cover: lyrics from the British Rock band Moody Blues and a Bible verse from John 10:7.

I don't know what I'm searching for,
I never have opened the door
Tomorrow may find me at last,
Turning my back on the past . . .

—Moody Blues, 1972

I am the door.

—Jesus Christ

Bob passed away in the late 1990s, but his words, dreams, and battles live on through his letters like kites flown to the future.

In one of Bob's letters, the one that starts with "another day in the life of a drug addict," Bob laments that he's not doing anything to help the "young black brothers and sisters."

I'm sharing your grandfather Bob's letters with you—they were given to me by Nna—because I think Bob's earnest letters to God are instructive, powerful, and capable of helping those young "brothers and sisters" that he wanted to help, but couldn't because his addiction turned him into what Uzi calls an "astronaut man." Bob passed before you were born, but I don't think he ever imagined that you or anyone would one day read his words, yet here we are, two generations and nine shots later.

**I'm too high strung to meditate**
**Feel the hurt I gotta medicate***

It's interesting that two years before Bob started his letters, on July 20, 1969, NASA astronaut Neil Armstrong landed on the moon and famously declared "One small step for man, one giant leap for mankind." I feel that sentiment when I think of your grandfather's letters. He didn't think much of his letters or himself at the time, however he felt, deep down, that he had a greater purpose on earth and that writing his words and experience might help someone, someday. And somehow, someway, his words find us now like faith in the abyss of darkness.

The French writer Albert Camus once said that "The purpose of a writer is to keep civilization from destroying itself." Bob's letters—many of them written under the moonlight while high on heroin—are testimonies against self-destruction. My hope is that they will help steer our family from the fangs of self-destruction. Armstrong later explained that the Apollo moon mission showed the world we are not "forever chained to this planet and our

---

* Uzi, "24 Hourz," *The Nephew Soundtrack*, 2024.

visions go rather further than that and our opportunities are unlimited." The letters may have been a small step for Bob, but they were a giant step for us.

Sunday, June 13, 1971

Dear God,

Here's my situation as it stands now: been in Buffalo five years this July 4th, a little way from graduating, no income coming in other than cashing bad checks, borrowing from anybody and everybody, stealing from the gym, from my girl, from people's rooms on campus, no job, no home.

I've had the opportunity to make a lot of contacts that might be helpful later on in life but most people probably only have negative memories about me. Thoughts about a guy who God has given a lot of ability and talent and who hasn't taken advantage of, just wasting his life away really.

All I've done is inject something into the veins of my body that gives me an excuse to cop out. All dope to me is a means to an end and that end is self-destruction.

I really don't think that good things are supposed to happen to me. I don't think that I'm worthy. Ugly duckling. I'm someone who knows he has ability but who probably doesn't have the confidence and courage to put those abilities to the test.

I once heard it said that "a man who is afraid of being laughed at is a man who will never succeed." Capricorns are supposedly afraid to take risks. Getting back to injecting that poison into my veins.

I liked to get as high as I possibly could because getting high would give an avenue of escape from the reality of my struggle with myself.

**Paid in full, nobody speaks on what the cost is**
**Escaping self-hate is that what the cause is?** *

---

* Uzi, "NASA," *The Nephew Soundtrack*, 2024.

Dope provided the biggest longest suicidal avenues that I have ever come across. The feeling so good it makes you feel that you can kick all of your problems with no sweat, and since I like to make things hard for myself, dope was appealing because you can continue to partake every day, your body hollers for it.

It seems to me also that this is a one-way avenue because personally, I'm very seldom satisfied. I always want more but I have to be careful in this description because I don't want to put too much blame on the drug. Like I said earlier, it's only a means to an end. The real problem is me and what I think of myself. How I perceive myself in relationship to the rest of the world.

—Bob

# 11 / On the Frontlines

I sneak a peek at the trauma bay at Temple and it's a sea of red. The room feels like a war zone and that's probably because our city, with semiautos and ghetto bird helicopters hawking outside, is in the haze of war. The cold metal trays and tools, hot crimson splatter, and explosive chaos all remind me of something Nna says about family. "Families are minefields. We shimmy and sashay through them, knowing that, at any given movement, BOOM!"

You are nowhere in sight, but I know you're close, I know you're fighting. I keep pacing, it's hard to be still. Writing this letter is the only thing that sits me down. My pops always says, "if you want to write, sit your ass down and write."

Doctor Walker comes through the double doors in a slow stride. I can't hear everything he says, but I catch "coma" clearly. Collective gasps pour out in the lobby as he explains away.

". . . slow the metabolism . . . . blood flow . . . pressure." He keeps talking but I am stuck on the word "coma."

Even though I know your big brown lids are shut, my chorus for you still marches on.

"Fight!"

"Nephew!"

"Fight . . ."

"Rumble that, Nephew!"

In the lobby, new faces appear but their grimace is the same. I hear chatter of revenge, of getting back, of retaliation. Tension rising like temperatures. Street soldiers in black Air Force 1s ready to pay it back in blood. I feel their rage. My blood boils when I think about who did this to you. Elders sigh and shake their heads at the never-ending cycle of what is to come. When will it end? The late Palestinian writer Edward Said once wrote, "You cannot continue to victimize someone else just because you yourself were a victim once."

> Mom worried about me, I'm moving too fast
> She don't wanna get a call from the district
> Thinking she going have to bury me
> I'm on the path to be another statistic*

I reflect back on the road, back to your flow. As I listen to your music on the ride up here, I feel the frequency morphing into something ominous. I hear the sounds of warfare and feel the blood splattering across the 808s. But it's not just the

---

* Neph, "Wat3R," *The Nephew Soundtrack*, 2024.

bloodthirsty beat that's at battle, I can hear the warfare in your lyrics.

> My niggas demons
> Run on your block for no reason
> Ain't stopping 'til somebody bleeding
> Or somebody momma is screaming*

As I watch your mom sob in the hospital—along with all the other mothers, their faces in puddles—I realize that you don't truly understand the power and prophecy in your poetry. I know that because I know how much you love your own mother—infinitely! So when you rhyme "somebody momma is screaming," I don't feel that, can't feel that because that's not you. That line isn't a reflection of your light. You are the kid who just sacrificed his life for others. Your mom can't cosign that either. She's in the lobby now going off about the violence in the city.

"Too many of our children are being murdered in the streets," she cries out. Grandma Beverly nods in pain. "We can't even send our children to trick or treat without fear of them being shot. Our kids can't even have a childhood anymore . . ."

I feel *her* heartbeat in her words.

"I don't have all the answers but one thing I know is that I can't turn a blind eye on what's happening in Philly. If you're not a part

---

* Neph, "Hitta," *The Nephew Soundtrack*, 2024.

of the solution then you're a part of the problem. Everyone in this city has lost someone to gun violence."

Your mom's passion and authenticity remind me of Fannie Lou Hamer speaking on the conditions of her time. Hamer, a powerful black woman from Mississippi, was a former sharecropper who stood up to oppression. She is the cofounder of the Mississippi Freedom Democratic Party (MFDP) and, in 1964, traveled to the Democratic National Convention to demand that the MFDP's delegates be seated in the convention.

"All of this is on account we want to register, to become first-class citizens, and if the freedom Democratic Party is not seated now, I question America, is this America, the land of the free and the home of the brave where we have to sleep with our telephones off of the hooks because our lives be threatened daily because we want to live as decent human beings, in America?"

Hamer's testimony is so powerful, so biting in its truth, that President Lyndon Johnson called an impromptu press conference to get her off the air.

Hamer is tired of the waiting game, tired of watching the slaughter. She says, "We been waitin' all our lives, and still getting killed, still getting hung, still getting beat to death. Now we're tired waitin'!"

That same year, Hamer joins Malcolm X on the stage in Harlem and gives a speech called "I'm sick and tired of being sick and tired."

And that's what I see in your mom: a beautiful authentic Black woman who is "sick and tired of being sick and tired."

You are a poet, a bearer of light. Be careful and deliberate with your words. Be surgical with your pen, treating your words with the care and intention that I pray the doctors show you now.

Prophecy is the proud parent of poetry. Through your rhymes, listeners can peak through the blinds into tomorrow. Your music is a powerful force in designing your reality and future. Harriet Tubman isn't writing and singing about freedom so that she can remain enslaved, but so that she can manifest freedom for herself and others. Lyrics, like the countless prayers being sent up to the heavens for you now, possess the incredible power to manifest. Rapping is manifestation.

When I first hear that you are shot, I think of the lyrics from one of Uzi's songs, "Yada." He spits:

> Spent my prime doing time, turned diesel Optimus
> No father figures so them bullets they be poppin' us[*]

It's such a chilling, devasting line because it illustrates his awareness. Sometimes bad decisions are made in ignorance—someone not knowing—but Uzi's bars show he is far from ignorant. His profound, prophetic lyrics air out just how aware he is of his actions and the consequences they have on all of us. It's like when

---

[*]   Uzi, "Yada," *The Nephew Soundtrack*, 2024.

Nna scolds, "you know better," or Auntie Maya saying "When you know better, do better."

So the question now, Nephew, since you, too, know better, is what are you manifesting, through your lyrics, for yourself? For your mom and little sister? For your little cousins? For the young bucks on your beloved block that look up to you?

**I'm just a messenger, the actual to factual**
**Funerals are formals but homicide is casual**
**Mother say, "my baby ain't never hurt nobody"**
**But the brothers know your baby was out here catching bodies***

The shooting plus the death I hear swirling in your bars make me think of our lineage of beloved rap poets—from 2Pac to Nipsey Hussle—and the prophecy they manifested. I hear their voices in your music and I hear your voice in theirs.

Wednesday, June 16, 1971

Dear God,

Today was the first day I got high since Sunday night. Seems like I can't refrain from getting high one way or another.

Strange things are happening to me. I don't know what I'm doing. I'm not putting any hard work into anything. I should ask myself some questions: Do I want to continue in school here in Buffalo or anywhere? What good is a college ed now? Is psychology important to Black people?

I'm not doing anything right to stay off drugs, Jefferson Ave, and anywhere else there are drugs.

---

* Uzi, "Sob Story," *The Nephew Soundtrack*, 2024.

**OG, Philly Blunts, OE, Jefferson Street,**
**Bodied over bottles of that purple yellow codeine***

I'm broke and in the hole now, I think I have a job. I'm hurting myself. When am I going to stop? What's wrong? Why don't I do what's right? Be a man and grow up before it's too late.

I'm afraid to face reality and take care of business and do things to the best of my ability. Why don't I see things as they are? I'm throwing my life away and all the things God has given me, I've not taken advantage of. Why am I so afraid? Please God help me to do things right and to be good. Guide me in my daily decisions, actions. Cleanse my mind and thoughts. Help me be a strong person + good people. My first order of priority is to stay away and completely off drugs. Let's get it together. Let's not waste any more time or waste any more of my God given gifts.

Life is a gift from God and we must not abuse it. God help me.

—Bob

---

\* Uzi, "NASA," *The Nephew Soundtrack*, 2024.

# 12 / Manifest

The manifestation, just like the music, is real. I remember when I was in Gujarat, India, reading a Gandhi quote on the wall where I taught at the MICA School of Ideas: "Keep your thoughts positive, because your thoughts become your words. Keep your words positive, because your behaviors become your habits. Keep your habits positive, because your habits become your values. Keep your values positive, because your values become your destiny." This speaks to the manifestation in our words, lyrics. Auntie Maya says, "Ask for what you want and be prepared to get it." Think about how this wisdom and awareness may have been able to save some of our most beloved rappers from their premature demises.

Tupac Amaru Shakur, aka 2Pac (June 16, 1971–September 13, 1996), released the ominous song "If I Die 2Nite" just a year before he was shot four times and killed in Las Vegas.

> I hope they bury me and send me to my rest
> Headlines readin' "Murdered to Death," my last breath*

---

* 2Pac, "If I Die 2Nite," *Me Against the World*, 1996.

Christopher Wallace, aka Notorious B.I.G., aka Biggie (May 21, 1972–March 9, 1997), releases the dark song "Suicidal Thoughts" on the album *Ready to Die* before his murder in Los Angeles.

> The stress is buildin' up, I can't believe
> I swear to God I feel like death is fuckin' callin' me*

Lamont Coleman aka "Big L" (May 30, 1974–February 15, 1999) releases the fateful song "Casualties of a Dice Game" the same year of his murder in his hometown of Harlem.

> I got weak and fell on my rear
> Now I can hear the sirens, that means here
> Comes the Jakes, But it's too late,
> I'm knocking on the pearly gates†

DeShaun Dupree Holton aka Proof (October 2, 1973–April 11, 2006) releases the foreshadowing song "40 Oz" two years before his murder at the CCC nightclub on Eight Mile Road in his hometown of Detroit.

> I'm in the club to beef
> You gotta murder me there‡

Airmiess Joseph Asghedom aka Nipsey Hussle (August 15, 1985–March 31, 2019) makes "Welcome Home" the same year of

---

\* Notorious B.I.G., "Suicidal Thoughts," *Ready to Die*, 1997.
† Big L, "Casualties of a Dice Game," *The Big Picture*, 1999.
‡ D12, "40 Oz," *D12 World*, 2004.

his murder in the parking lot of his store, The Marathon Clothing Store, in his hometown South Central, LA.

> Gave my mind to these millions
> And my heart to the game
> Probably die up in these streets
> But I survive through my name*

Our dear brother, Nip. How can I express a river with a tear? His departure hits me like a death in the family.

> I never planned to make it to a old nigga
> Plant the bag, 560 off a zone, nigga†

In his eulogy for Nip, Minister Farrakhan remarks, "He lived the gang life, but he didn't stay there. He lived the life of the hood, but he rose above the pull of gravity."

As you lay in a cold coma in the valley of the shadow of death, I change my ER chorus. Fight becomes rise.

"Rise, Nephew! Rise!"

Rise out of this hospital bed, rise above the ignorance that threatens you, rise out of the cycle of poverty and recklessness, rise over self-destruction, rise above the heat of gun smoke, above the dust of death, above the self-hatred, above your past, above the

---

* The Game featuring Nipsey Hussle, "Welcome Home," *Born to Rap*, 2019.
† Nipsey Hussle, "Crenshaw & Slauson (True Story)," *Crenshaw*, 2013.

jungle with its snakes, rats, pigs, above it all. I think of my mentor, Auntie Dr. Maya Angelou's famous refrain:

> Just like moons and like suns,
> With the certainty of tides,
> Just like hopes springing high,
> Still I'll rise.

Nna loves Auntie Maya Angelou and when I made the film *The Black Candle* with her, I put them both in the movie together, side by side. Many years ago, in 1976, when Uzi is two years old, Bob gives Nna the book *Singin' and Swingin' and Gettin' Merry Like Christmas* by Maya Angelou and signs it, "Sing and swing to make a merry Xmas!"

August 20, 1971

Dear God,

Tuesday I was scheduled to be sentenced for soliciting for the purpose of obtaining drugs, a Class B misdemeanor. Since I pleaded guilty the charge was reduced from a Class A misdemeanor, which is possession of a dangerous drug. The sentencing was postponed because I failed to keep my appointment with my probation officer.

A cat can say that he's a dope fiend and be sent to a rehab instead of jail. Since this is my first conviction, I'll probably be given probation. The sentence is a class B misdemeanor with a first offense of 3 months to a max of 5 months. The problem is that if you are declared a dope fiend it goes on your record. Now it's bad enough to have a police record, but to have it say you shoot dope is even worse.

**First came smack, then came base**
**On attack, it's been destroying my race**

Whether skeletal face or a federal case
From summit to plummet at an incredible pace*

As always Carole went out of her way to try to help me.

Carole came to court to support me.

When we left, she told me to hold her briefcase, which contains papers for her. The first thing I did was go into it and see if there was a check in it, and sure enough there was. I took four of them out, put the checkbook back in the case, and closed up the case. This wasn't a stranger that I stole from, but the woman I'm supposed to love—for dope money.

I've written bad checks to people I've known ever since I've been up here, stolen from people at the gym, stolen money from Carole, cashed checks for money that was not only Carole's, but the other members of the Black Dance Workshop.

I'm messing with something that if I don't have it, it won't permit me to remove waste materials from my body, won't permit me to eat, make love, be with my woman, play ball, go to school, go to work, walk, talk, and think. This is what I've done to myself. There was a time when I used to think about going out with Carole, about playing ball, about going to school, about making love to Carole, about marrying her. Now I don't think about anything really but how am I going to get some money to buy dope. Where am I going to buy it from? Will it be good? Is it dope or a dummy? And as soon as I do get over, where am I going to get some more.

Dear God why do I make trouble for myself like this. People even at the gym know I'm the one who has been stealing people's money and watches.

It seems like I'm not happy unless I create some sort of problem. Don't I ever want good things to happen to me? Don't I ever want to be happy? Don't I ever want to be doing good? If I really can't look people in the face because I

---

*   Uzi, "NASA", *The Nephew Soundtrack*, 2024.

know I'm not doing what's right. If someone asks me now what am I doing all I could say is I shoot dope, steal from my woman and anybody else I can, lie to get money from anyone, and play ball every once in a while. So this what life is about, so this what you put me on earth to do?

God please forgive me for what I've done, what I've been doing is wrong. Please help me be strong.

People haven't pressed any charges against me yet, but if I keep going on like this I'll run into somebody who will and then I'll end up in jail where I can't do anything.

I'm 25 yrs. old now and I'm not getting any younger. I want to enjoy my life and dope is only misery.

I want to do good. In my moments of weakness, please let me remember what I've written here, please help me think that things could be so much better than they are now and not life as a dope fiend getting high. So very much more. I'll talk to you later.

—Bob

# 13 / Food of the System

Uzi gets knocked again and goes back to jail in 2008. This time he goes to CFCF on State Road in Philly. The design of the prison industrial complex is a revolving door. You know how it goes; going in, coming home, repeat. Of course, he's been *in* before, but this time is different for Uzi, for all of us.

**We the food of the system, yo free the akhis**
**State browns and them greens, we beef and broccoli***

One difference is that Uzi starts writing rhymes again while he's inside. Every call from jail he's spitting acapella to me. As he raps, I can hear that "noise," that "constant roar like hard wind blowing into your ear" in the background. Uzi spits hard like he's trying to win an argument. A familiar fire in his bars.

"Listen to this," he says, then snaps: "I say . . ."

**Apache Polo's I'm snappy in tacky logos**
**Po-po's come at me with scratchy photos**

---

* Uzi, "Open Bar," *The Nephew Soundtrack*, 2024.

> Judge with a grudge makes sure the sentence sticks
> So we just get sent up—incense sticks

I get hype and give him energy when he rhymes. Even incarcerated, it's beautiful to see him embrace one of his many gifts and tell his story in verse.

> This is for my soldiers in wayward placements
> Locked down pits left to pace in basements
> Jury selling jewels adjacent bracelets
> Can't live but can't die you just wasting patience

He shares the lyrics to a song called "Sob Story." He makes the beat by banging on a metal tray and stomping the concrete.

> This for my people up-top on State Road
> Who ain't never gettin' out after the first gate fold
> 25 with a L, the hurt his face told,
> killed a cat under the El trying to take his fake gold*

His jail calls remind me of my childhood, when he would ring our jack from jail in Arizona. This is back in 'ninety-one. The Gulf War in Iraq is just starting. I remember they interrupt the Bulls vs. Magic game—in the middle of a Jordan fadeaway—to show President George H. Bush's announcement: "As I report to you, air attacks are under way against military targets in Iraq . . . I've told the American people before that this will not be another Vietnam." Uzi's jail time feels like war.

---

* Uzi, "Sob Story," *The Nephew Soundtrack*, 2024.

Old sneaks, winter time, cold feet
Get knocked, it's a rap, no beat
It's a war going on, the niggas and the cops
Death or detention, as long as it's a box*

I'm ten years old at the time and, when I reflect, I ain't been the same since. Shit crushes me; to see my big brother in shackles. A lonely chaos follows his sentence like storm clouds. It's an era of fog for our fam. I remember Nna's reaction:

*If I could run, hide from bad news, I would be on the other side of the world. Bad news has ridden the hem of my skirts and I haven't been able to dance the news away. Now bad news has arrived big time and in this midnight hour, when everyone is asleep and only the TV talks, I am speechless but full of fear. Fear for my child. The one that I put on the plane a little over a year ago. The child that I wanted to save and didn't know what to do. My firstborn child who was full of life and too much mischief. He was in jail facing what?*

The only slice of blue sky are his calls from jail. Uzi only writes me one letter from jail, but he calls at least once a week. Those collect calls are my lifeline.

I stay near the house phone (imagine, haha—a phone on a cord), answering every call, waiting for that one monotone voice to announce, "You have a collect call from an inmate . . ." Then I smash the pound key to accept.

---

\* Uzi, "Sob Story," *The Nephew Soundtrack*, 2024.

"Yo!" He says, feeling out the connection. His voice is deep fresh water.

"Yo, Uzi!" I can't contain my excitement.

"What's Philly listening to?" He always asks from two thousand miles away.

While Uzi's locked up in Arizona, I am his Philly music ambassador and it's an honor. Once a week after school I go to Uptown Flava on Eleventh and Market with my boys Jon and Jessie. There we listen to the latest DJ Clue or Cosmic Kev mixtapes. I cop DJ Clue's *Blizzard* mixtape, which introduces me to Biggie, Canibus, and Nas.

"This new boy named Nas," I say.

"Nas?"

"Yeah, Nasty Nas from Queens Bridge, he's on the new DJ Clue tape." Clue is my favorite DJ back then because he always debuts new MCs like Nas, Fabolous, and Canibus. I pull the tangled mustard-colored cord from the Bell Atlantic phone toward my boom box because I know what's coming . . .

"Let me hear that shit!" Not a request, but a demand!

> Straight out the fucking dungeons of rap
> where fake nghs don't make it back, it's time*

---

* Nas, "N.Y. State of Mind," *Illmatic*, 1994.

I put the phone firmly against the speaker.

The drums from DJ Premier's "N.Y. State of Mind" beat slap so hard I can hear Uzi say, "Damn." I hear him call other inmates over, like, *Yo, Y'all gotta hear this right now!* I can hear the crowd in the background as they gather around the phone. Now I'm the official DJ for Arizona State Prison—yeah!

**I got so many rhymes, I don't think I'm too sane**
**Life is parallel to Hell, but I must maintain***

"Turn that shit up," someone yells in the background. But the volume is to the max. My staticky Sanyo speakers struggle to keep up. I push the phone into the speaker so hard I dent the cheap aluminum grill.

"It's up!" I yell back, but they can't even hear me. The whole song is cinematic. Nas's hero-tone voice commands our focus be singular. I hear Uzi and the inmates going buck, apeshit, bananas.

**And be prosperous, though we live dangerous, cops could just**
**Arrest me, blaming us, we're held like hostages†**

They react to Nas's bars as if they were NBA dunks. I hear the clink boom clank of Black fists beating on stone and metal. I can feel their heads nodding, their arms flying in approval and solidarity.

---

*† Nas, "N.Y. State of Mind," *Illmatic*, 1994.

Inhale deep like the words of my breath
I never sleep, cause sleep is the cousin of death*

Even over an unstable prison phone line, Nas's lines are crystal clear. I'm in middle school yelling "free all my nghs locked down" and telling Uzi to "keep his head up." Nna calls me "Manchild" and gives me a book called *Manchild in the Promised Land* by Claude Brown.

They stir the pain and the trauma in the tonic
Jail phone DJ played "Illmatic" and "Chronic"
Phone to receiver of a staticky speaker
Had my big bro cell block jumping like lemurs†

Those moments between me and Uzi—miles, years, and realities apart—show me the power of music; to connect, heal, and transform.

Years later, Nna tells me about the time she choreographed and debuted a dance for Bob on TV while he was in jail. Assata says, "Love is the acid that eats away bars."

\*\*\*

September 10, 1971

Dear God,
    Dope is so dehumanizing. It prevents me from playing ball cause my body feels so bad sometimes. I don't want to be with my woman 'cause I'd rather nod along

---

\* Nas, "N.Y. State of Mind," *Illmatic*, 1994.
† MK Asante, "Brown Stew Snapper," *The Nephew Soundtrack*, 2024.

and enjoy the high. With her I have to fight the high and that causes other problems. As far as I've seen, the disadvantages far outweigh the advantages. How long will I go on like this?

I really look forward to the day when I won't need drugs for any purpose to get high. To go to sleep or anything. Dope hasn't done anything for me but make problems. But like I said I'm my worst enemy. God, you have given me a lot of talent and ability and I've done everything in my power to destroy that talent.

I'm doing nothing for me and everything against me. Drugs are only putting me in a hole. Maybe I should leave Buffalo, but not without getting this monkey off of my back.

> **Bought the monkey on my back a pair J's**
> **I got a fresh conscience**
> **Come dine at the table of my contents** *

Carol has a concert this Sunday. We love each other very much and we could have such a beautiful thing if only I would get myself together. Here she is doing so very much for herself and others while I get high. I could have done so much since I've been here but I would rather cop out. We could have been married by now and have something instead of bullshitting.

What if she doesn't love me now as much as she used to? That would be a blow. God has given me so much and I waste so much.

I have to stop lying to myself and everyone else. It doesn't serve any purpose. It only hinders my development and growth. When am I going to grow up and be a man? But as the song goes, "A man is hard to be." Especially being a black man. What I should do is do everything that I'm afraid to do.

---

* MK Asante x Uzi, "Bangers (remix)," *The Nephew Soundtrack*, 2024.

I do know that dope is no good and I must cut it loose. Life means more than just a high. It's nation time.

**the black man is the future of the world**

**be come**

**rise up**

**It's Nation Time***

We learn from the past and use lessons we learn in the future. Everyone makes mistakes. I'm going to give it my best so help me God. Talk to you later.

—Bob

---

\* Amiri Baraka, "It's Nation Time," *It's Nation Time - African Visionary Music,* 1972.

# 14 / The Victorious One

"Why Nasir?" I ask your mom one day as I drop you off at Macedonia Free Will Baptist church. I'm curious because I know one of Uzi's favorite rappers is Nas, but I also know he wasn't around to name you. Also, your mom is a devout Christian and Nasir is an Arabic name popular among Muslims; it means "the victorious one."

**Times I remember,**
**Mama always said I'm a winner[*]**

"Escobar," your mom says with an instant smile. "Nas Escobar, Nasir Jones, Esco was always my favorite rapper." She lights up when she talks about hip-hop back in the day, being an Uptown Philly girl, baggy airbrushed clothes, house parties, Nas. She goes on to tell me how "Hassan," your middle name, comes from her brother. Hassan means good in Arabic and Imam Hassan was the grandson of the prophet Muhammad.

**That's right, you know my name I got the devil on the run**
**Why? Cause my motherfuckin Uzi weighs a ton[†]**

---

[*] Neph, "R3M3MBA," *The Nephew Soundtrack*, 2024.
[†] Jay Electronica, "My Uzi Weighs a Ton," *What the Fuck Is a Jay Electronica*, 2011.

"Hassan is my little brother's name and we are the closest. Growing up we fought each other sometimes and other people all the time. Once I saw him fight, and realized he couldn't, I always jumped in all his fights. I never let anyone pick on him."

As you lay in a coma with doctors scrambling to save your life and loving hands clasped together in prayer for you, I take comfort in knowing that the fight in your mom is the same fight in you. And I know you will take comfort in knowing that your heroic actions saved the lives of your little cousins.

\*\*\*

October 31, 1971

Dear God,

Before we even get down to Jefferson Ave and Ferry, light skin Anthony who plays over at the Boys Club sometimes was driving down Jefferson and when he saw it was me, he pulled over. I thought he was going to give Tom and me a ride down Jefferson but instead he said that the brother who was in the car with him had a nice thing. Anthony's always been up and up with me, so I took his word that everything was everything. So I copped four things and Anthony gave Tom and me a ride back to Tom's crib. We did that and it was so-so. Getting high, once again, is getting to be a drag.

Fiends chase the initial high, no aces
Feast on the streets, prey on food, no graces
Lost souls running loose no laces
When they feel deserted, the high's an oasis\*

---

\*  Uzi, "NASA," *The Nephew Soundtrack*, 2024.

I'm splitting now to go up to the Freedom School for a minute, so I'll be right back.

I think it's a sin to spend $80, $85, and $90 a day on a dope habit. Shooting something into my body that doesn't last that long. It would be different if it was medicine that I needed to sustain my life, like insulin for diabetes. All dope does is damage.

This guy who's black, about 25 years old, 6'3". He left his home because he felt that his relatives were taking advantage of him. He had no alternative. Anyway, he works for about three years in the city before coming to Buffalo. He is intelligent, fairly good-looking, athletic. I'm trying to create a comparable situation so that I can see what I look like in my present stage. Let's say a guy going to school, playing ball, working and making good money, has a nice crib, a nice girl and . . . he throws it all away for dope.

How would he look upon a person who seemingly has given up everything? Sold his car, wore the same clothes for almost two months, stopped seeing his woman, stopped making love to her, stopped playing ball, his appearance changed drastically. Sometimes he wouldn't brush his teeth or comb his hair or take a shower for a period at a time, who became a thief. How long can he live like that? Writing checks for money that not only is not his, but that's not his woman's either, but belongs to a group that his woman is a member of, so it's all of their money. He owes them a lot. God has watched over him in many instances like the time he took an overdose of CIBA's (benzoctamine), he could have died but for some reason he didn't die.

—Bob

# 15 / Inshallah

When Uzi goes to jail, both in the 1990s and in the 2000s, the calls always begin and end the same way.

"Salamalekum," he affirms in Arabic. Uzi finds Islam in jail like a lot of brothers do. Malcolm X went from street hustler Malcolm Little to Brother Malcolm X while incarcerated at Charlestown State Prison in Boston.

"I had sunk to the very bottom of the American white man's society when—soon now, in prison—I found Allah and the religion of Islam and it completely transformed my life," writes X, who becomes El-Hajj Malik El Shabazz, in his autobiography with Alex Haley, *The Autobiography of Malcolm X*.

Studies show that the rate of recidivism among Muslims in prison is the lowest among any group. For Uzi and many others, Islam helps instill values of honesty, integrity, hard work, discipline, and alcohol/drug rehab.

**Streets is tryin to turn me otherly**
**Babymomma tuggin' me**

Off my deen, Mu'min (مؤمن)
So I scheme humbly*

Uzi's conversion is part of a rich spiritual tradition. NBA
Hall-of-Famer Kareem Abdul-Jabbar, born Lew Alcindor in 1947,
converts to Islam while leading UCLA to win three consecutive
National Championships. He says that "Malcolm X's transformation
from petty criminal to political leader inspired me to look more
closely at my upbringing and forced me to think more deeply about
my identity. Islam helped him find his true self and gave him the
strength not only to face hostility from both Blacks and whites but
also to fight for social justice. I began to study the Quran."

Let me talk to em just for a minute,
Let met talk to em just for a second
Wake up, Alhamdulillah (أَلْحَمْدُ لِلَّهِ), feeling blessings†

"Islam means peace," Uzi explains over the phone.

Islam builds Uzi a temple of hope and faith when he finds
himself in a place without it. This is remarkable when the approach
to faith is serious and studious.

I can hear from the lyrics in your music that you, like Uzi,
are also embracing Islam. I hear you sprinkling Arabic words like
"Astaghfirullah" (forgiveness), "Masjidullah" (house of God), and
"Inshallah" (God willing) in your raps.

---

* Uzi, "The Bulletin," *The Buck Soundtrack*, 2015.
† Neph, "For a Second," *The Nephew Soundtrack*, 2024.

Even though I be sinnin', I'm-a make Salat (صَلَاة)
And I'll die before I let you nghz take what I got
Started with a dollar and I'm-a make it a knot
Been through war, so much pain that I got*

I think it's truly beautiful that both you and Uzi, despite the distance, the absence, find Islam. Uzi's name, Daahoud, is Arabic and means "my beloved." Both of your names, Nasir and Hassan, are also Arabic, meaning "good" and "supporter."

As you explore Islam, please remember brother Malcolm's commitment to Islam. Remember Muhammad Ali, who explains "Allah's the Arabic term for God. Stand up for God, fight for God, work for God and do the right thing, and go the right way, things will end up in your corner."

When it should be a natural way of life
Who am I or they to say to whom you pray ain't right
That's who got you doing right and got you this far
Whether you say "in Jesus name" or "Hamdullah"†

I pray that one day Uzi considers not just the kind of Muslims Malcolm and Ali were, but also the kind of fathers they were—Malcolm to Malikah, Ilyasah, Gamilah, Malaak, Qubilah, and Attallah—and Ali to Muhammad Jr., Laila, Asaad, Rasheda, Hana, Maryum, Jamillah, Khaliah, and Miya.

* Neph, "Soul Right," *The Nephew Soundtrack*, 2024.
† "Common x CeeLo Green, G.O.D. (Gaining One's Definition)," *One Day It'll All Make Sense*, 1997.

In Islam, children are gifts from Allah.

In the Quran, which Uzi tells me he reads in jail, the prophet Muhammad writes, "The right of a child upon his father is that he should choose a good name for him, choose a good wet-nurse for him, and raise him well . . . Among the rights of a child upon his father is that he should properly upbring his child and does not deny his relation to him."

> All he got is Salat (صَلَاة)
> So God bless, man
> But God don't like ugly
> So we all must pay our debts, man

One passage that resonates with me, as your uncle, is Sunan al-Darimi, narrating from Shurhabil ibn Sa'd, who says: "Once Hasan gathered his children and his brother's children and said: O my children and my brother's children! You are the little young people of this generation and there is a hope that you will be the great ones of another generation. Therefore, learn knowledge, and he who cannot learn it by heart should write it down and keep it in his home."

I share these things with Uzi over the years during our conversations and the rare moments when I see him between jail stints.

"A lot of brothers in there would do anything to see their kids, bro," I say. "Never too late." I think about how hard some fathers have to fight—against stereotypes, courts, bitter baby mommas and exes, and a slanted system—just to be fathers.

How you tell a kid he won't eat?
Go to bed with a hoodie no heat*

One thing he is stuck on is the feeling that he doesn't have anything to offer. This is a distortion of his own gifts and talents—like someone with body dysmorphia who can't see what everybody else sees—because he has so much to offer; to you, to his family, and to the world. I think his mind is on the money. I share with him the words of Imam al-Sadiq who says, "The best thing that fathers could leave for their children as inheritance is manners, not wealth, for wealth perishes but manners remain."

We deens, yahmeen, schemes, my team
Yo, blessings, ameen†

Every time Uzi goes to jail, one of the things I pray for is for him to begin to take his faith, Islam—"Peace" in Arabic—seriously and actually practice what is preached. I deeply believe that if he does that, he will ignite a new paradigm of knowledge, wisdom, and understanding. A sense of long-awaited peace.

***

November 3, 1971

Dear God,

I'm sitting in Tom's house watching a TV program called *Chronolog* which was formerly called *First Tuesday*. The segment that's on now is about Oral Roberts

---

* Uzi, "Sob Story," *The Nephew Soundtrack*, 2024.
† MK Asante x Uzi, "Buck Shots," *The Buck Soundtrack*, 2015.

University in Tulsa, Oklahoma, which was started and presided over by the faith healing evangelist named Oral Roberts.

So it is only faith which is necessary for a person to be around.

I read an article today out of the magazine *Plain Truth*, which was dealing with heroin and its misconceptions and other information. Heroin has become the central part of my life. It's the first thing I think about when I wake up and usually the last thing on my mind at night. I do nothing else but try to get over.

How can I? I have no clothes, no money, and no woman, mainly because my mind is on drugs.

The article I was reading said that people who use drugs have character defects. In my case I think that's true because I've never thought too much of myself and I guess that's why I've done just about everything in my power to destroy every opportunity that you've given me. Because I don't think much of myself.

Right now I'm in a hole that I've dug myself in, which does not mean that I can't dig myself out of this hole. Something else will have to fill that void, which dope now occupies.

**White lines, nickels and dimes**

**In different declines, the minor constricting the binds**

**Chasing that first high trying to mimic it's climbs**

**Elders watch from windows and remember simpler times, huh***

There's something about dope that is almost unexplainable. It has a mystic hold on people. It becomes something that you want. That feeling you get when you get that "hit" is something else. You just want to have that feeling as much as you can. This probably explains why people do what they do, go thru so many changes as they do.

—Bob

---

* Uzi, "NASA," *The Nephew Soundtrack*, 2024.

# 16 / Imani

The doctors are in surgery. One of the surgeons gives your mom some papers to sign. They hand her some booklets and connect her with a social worker. I hear something about a 12 percent chance of survival. I zone out whenever the news is bleak. I hear it, but I don't feel it. My faith won't allow it in. I'm singing your song in my head, *No weapon . . . shall prosper . . . it won't work.*

Nephew, please continue to express your faith in your music and life. The purpose of music is to uplift our brothers and sisters, not destroy them. One of the first hip-hop songs ever made is called "The Message" for a reason. Growing up, Uzi loves Grandmaster Flash and the Furious Five, running around the house singing: *It's like a jungle sometimes / It makes me wonder / how I keep from goin' under.* Uzi carries a boom box around with him.

> A child is born with no state of mind
> Blind to the ways of mankind
> God is smiling on you, but he's frowning too
> Because only God knows what you'll go through*

---

* Grandmaster Flash and the Furious Five, "The Message," *The Message*, 1982.

Bring the message of peace, the very meaning of your faith, to the people. This is the part of your message that resonates with all faiths.

Hebrews 11:1 says, "Faith is the substance of things hoped for and the evidence of things not seen."

Nephew, this letter, right here, right now, is an act of faith. You can't open your eyes or hear anything right now, but I know you feel me like mirror-touch synesthesia.

Faith isn't over there or there, it's right here sitting under these fluorescent bulbs in Temple University Hospital's dingy lobby, ignoring their dire prognoses on your life, ignoring the death that encircles us, writing this to you with nine bullets in your eighteen-year-old body.

Faith isn't just penning this letter, but believing, with all my heart, that you will someday read it.

Faith is knowing that you will not only read it.

Faith　is　anticipating　your　response　.　.　.

December 27, 1971

Dear God,

Today was another day in the life of a drug addict. Only one thing on my mind, get over.

The most important thing is that I replace drugs with something else. Replace the artificial high of drugs with the natural high of life.

Ghetto song sings a sad song with his pops
Is you nodding in agreement or is you on them Suboxones?
Young boy, like damn, what's wrong with my pops?
Young boy had a trey on him as long as a wrap*

Slowly but surely I'm coming to the realization that I'm wasting the best years of my life now. Today was a beautiful day but I couldn't take advantage of it and enjoy it because my mind was preoccupied with one thought, "get some money together so that I could get some dope." The first thing on my mind this morning was Roger coming over to get us (Tom + myself) high, not "Thank God I'm alive to enjoy this beautiful day or what Carole and I are going to do today." No, those thoughts never enter into my mind. Only how I can get over.

What is life and what is the purpose of life? To be a bum? A wino? An alcoholic? A dope fiend? Or is it to take advantage of God-given gifts and possibly help other people?

To do right, weakness has to fall by the wayside and that's what I've done, fallen by the wayside. I'm not doing anything for anybody myself, Carole, the young black brothers and sisters. God, can I do right and be happy? Am I scared to be happy?

—Bob

---

\* Uzi, "Sob Story," *The Nephew Soundtrack*, 2024.

# 17 / The Language of God

It's morning and the lobby feels like mourning time. Heads and gazes tilted south as the sun grows over the city.

"He's still alive," your aunt reminds the weary, tired prayer warriors who have spent nights here. "He's still alive."

I try to keep my head up, but I feel the weight of bad news too. It feels like there is a fifty-pound dumbbell strapped to the back of my neck.

I step out the side of the hospital to call Nna, check on her and give her an update on your condition.

"He's in surgery mom and everybody's just praying and trying to stay positive," I say on the phone as I pace outside around the ER drop-off zone. Across the street, on Ontario, I look at the rotting plywood covering the windows and doors of abandoned row homes.

"Do they know who did it yet? Have they made any arrests?"

"Not yet, Mom, but people know. The streets talk."

I notice that even though the homes across the street are abandoned, their foundations are still strong. Good bones. The marrow in the memories prevents collapse. Preservation and restoration of life, land, liberty—this is the language of the rising sun.

I decide I'm not going to tell her about the 12-percent survival rate BS because that will worry her.

"How are you, Mom?"

She sighs a where-do-I-start sigh.

"Well, I can feel my health deteriorating . . . I've been through a lot. Myomectomy, caesarean, gall bladder, appendectomy, hernia, Achilles tendon, bowel obstruction, and the list goes on . . . but this MSA is different." Throughout my life, I've seen Nna's health struggles. As soon as I'm able to drive a car, as a teenager, I drive her to her doctor's appointments as she fights through the storm.

"You are so strong, mom."

"Strength is knowing that it's okay to be fragile sometimes. How's Grandma Beverly?"

"Staying strong like you . . . and fragile," I say with a smile.

She admires your grandma Beverly's strength, her recovery from cancer, and her unwavering support of her family.

"Give her a hug for me when you see her," Nna says.

Nna admires Beverly's faith as well. Last week I see Nna reading the Bible for the first time in my life.

"I've never been dogmatic. There is so much truth in the world," she says, reminding me of an Opoku proverb. He says "Wisdom is like a great big baobab tree; no one individual can embrace it."

Growing up, Nna teaches me to honor all faiths and pens the only prayer I know by heart growing up:

We call upon our ancestors
Far and near, new and ancient
    Mothers of our mothers
    Fathers of our fathers
    To bear witness
    To render mercy
    For the liberation
    And victory
    Of all people
    It is done
    Amen.

We pray now for your preservation and restoration as well as Nna's health.

"I know I don't have a whole lot of time left—"

"Mom! C'mon, don't say that—none of us know how much time we have."

"Well that's true, but we will all die at some point, at least in the physical—" My head shakes "no." It's hard to hear her talk about death.

"I told Nasir when he was down here that I want to go—when it's my time to go—in peace. I told him that for one, him and his father need to connect. I know it's not his fault and I know it's not on him to initiate this, but I've asked him to at least be open to it. It is my hope that one day his father will man up and reach out to him."

Nna tells me about a poem she writes a long time ago, but never shares with anyone.

"It's called Prayer," she says. I hear her rustling papers in the background. Where I'm standing, I see two ambulances rush up.

Nna's airy, soft soprano starts reading:

I do not know whether to
            Look up or to bow down
When I pray to you my God
I do not know whether to turn
                East or west
            As I make myself heard
                Divine Creator
            Shall I cast
My hands out before me
                Or prostrate
            My body unto the floor

Seeking submission into the
Earth
I do not know whether to
Count three, six or nine
As I turn my cheek
Right and then left
Not knowing whether to
Lower my eyes
Or to let the depths of my soul
Penetrate the air
Helping to deliver my message.
Shall I speak to you my God
And submit to thy will?
Will you take me
As I come
Head covered or shoulder bare
Trembling or steadfast
While I utter my
Prayer
With cadences and breath
That belie
My intense belief in you?
If I could know what corner
Of the world
You are supposed to exist in
Or what manner
Is most perfect in which to address
I do not know how best
To present myself
While forming

My lips
To call
You

Lord
Allah
Jehovah
Buddha
Krishna

Or

simply

Olorun

Shall I come to you

on my knees

Or spread on a cross

Dipped in Baptismal waters

Or my forehead pressed to the earth

ALL is the same in my heart

My God

Exists for me

In ALL times

And ALL places

And ALL shapes and

ALL forms

And ALL spaces

And I being

Of one constant form

Can only conjure up

Images

while I stay put

To do

God's work
And man's love
And God's love
And man's work.
I do not now know whether
To speak in tongues
As I search for
The language
Of God
Whether to
Bend from the waist
Or to form the words Amen
A thousand times
And seek my salvation
I know my God
That I speak from
My heart and soul
And
Any manner of movement
Or form of my form
Are mere
Translations
Of a prayer
That will not yield
To interpretation
I pray that
You accept my prayer
In its humility
And I shall bow before you
While standing tall
Looking neither East nor West

                    North or south
Hands outstretched
                    To the four winds
And I will know
                    That I have been heard.
I know that I cannot
          Be all things
So I submit myself
              To the one truth
That there is a GOD
              One universal wisdom
                    And my history can
              Neither correct or deny
              That knowledge
I know that
          My prayer will
              Travel from
My lips each day
          To many messengers
And to one God
          And I know this
As I know myself
          To breathe
          And my God to exist
I offer myself in prayer
          AMEN.


                                        January 19, 1972

Dear God,
    Stealing, thieving, hiding from people, relying on others to get me high. God
can this crisis pass? If it does, I promise you I'll try my best never to do anything

wrong again and I'll try to steer people away from the temptations. Working with youth groups and just personal encounters. God, this I promise you. Believe me please help me.

In my life, I can't keep hiding from people. The rest of my life, I can't keep lying to people for the rest of my life and I can't live off other people for the rest of my life.

I've used up all my friends. Taken advantage of them, used them in situations when I really didn't need them, so now who can I turn to? Carole told me that someday when I really need someone to do a favor for me I won't have anyone to turn to because I've already used up all my favors on bullshit. I didn't believe her but I see what she means now. You always learn something too late, but I guess the secret of life is learning early.

I've lost my girlfriend, my apartment, my opportunity to obtain enough college credits to be near graduation if not graduation already (I was supposed to graduate if I had adhered to the regular time table in May 1971 because I started college in the summer of 1967 with the Upward Bound Program), my job with model cities, my willingness and ability to play basketball, my sex urge because when you're on dope you don't be thinking about making love, my health (I've lost considerable weight), all due to dope (heroin, scag, boy, beast, stuff, white knight or whatever you want to call it).

> No matter what the name, it's the same, under the moon
> It's as sad as the face staring at the flame, under the spoon
> Nghs pumping in doom so they can be stuntin' in June
> What about the single mother slumped, up in her room*

---

\* Uzi, "NASA," *The Nephew Soundtrack*, 2024.

What I really think is the problem is that I don't think I'm worthy of anything, that I don't deserve anything. That's a wrong attitude because with that attitude I'll never accomplish anything.

After I ate dinner, I went to the Boys Club on National, which isn't too far from Tom's house, to play ball. Even though my team won every game all night I really didn't contribute that much. Right now I play at about ¼ of my ability, and that's mainly due to drugs and not playing. My body is weak, very weak. Drugs don't make your body strong. How can I play ball when my mind is on something else? Thinking about something else, my body is telling me to get that dope. Do anything but get that dope! A change has got to come.

If somebody took something from my room or apartment and I knew who did it there are three possible courses of action—call the police and have a warrant put out for us, do us bodily harm, or beat us up or shoot us (Bill may have a gun from what I understand, even though I don't know what he intends to do with it).

—Bob

# 18 / Still Water Runs Deep

The other reason why Uzi's incarceration is different this time is—

"My girl is pregnant," Uzi tells me on a jail call. His release date from jail is after the baby's due date. It's confusing for me because the reason he's in jail, this time, is because of a domestic incident with his girl, Danielle. They get into it, *yadda-yadda woop-woop*.

When Nna finds out about the pregnancy from Uzi's phone call, she sends Danielle a letter:

September 28, 2010

Dear Danielle,

I hope that you and the children are fine. Daudi has called me from jail to ask that you take the restraining order off him. I don't have your phone number or I would call you. Whatever you two agree to in terms of your relationship, it is probably not a good idea to have him in jail. Daudi says that he will go to a shelter if you don't want him to return to Pearl Street. I don't have any other information from him. You can always call me if you need to.

Take care,

Mama K (Nna)

With Uzi in jail and Danielle pregnant, I think about you, Nephew; his absence in your life, and of course, about the fate of my new nephew. I wonder what his name will be. If my brother, once he gets out, will be there for him.

> Baby momma broke, she movin to the next man
> No more letters, no more cheddar, you the x-man
> Shank in his fist, Wolverine, he a x-man
> Thorazine—he contemplating death, man[*]

A few weeks later, Nna calls in the middle of the night. Calls in the middle night are almost always bad, so I am relieved and excited to hear Nna's tone.

"She's in labor, she's in labor."

> New jails, new cells cuz the plan man is F - ya!
> Courtesy of the brotherly, sunny in the ugly
> Bummy is that Coventry, money for that crumbly
> Govy wanna number me[†]

I jump in the S5 and race over to Chestnut Hill Hospital where Danielle's having the baby. It's Chestnut Hill Hospital, so you can probably guess who's working at the hospital that night.

At the time I didn't know your grandma Beverly works the front desk at Chestnut Hill. I walk up to the front and it feels

---

like I'm in a dream. I'm here to watch my brother's 2nd child, my 2nd nephew, come into the world, and the receptionist is Grandma Beverly, who's been trying to get Uzi to be a father to his firstborn.

> Cell so cold, you make that bed
> That's where you rest, man
> Be a king or a pawn in the system,
> Life is chess, man*

She recognizes me and we embrace. She sits back down and it looks like she's floating, a peaceful buoyancy about her. I explain to her that I'm here to see the birth of my second nephew. I can see her thinking, *where's your brother?*

"My brother is locked up," I tell her.

"I'm sorry hear to hear that." I can see her doing some math in her head. "Did he get my letter?"

Feeling shame for my brother's absence, I nod, smile, and cut to the elevator.

Upstairs, your baby brother, another gift from God, is born healthy and linebacker-huge at almost twelve pounds. From jail, Uzi names him Fukai, which means still, deep water in Japanese.

Fukai's birth is the first birth that I ever witness.

---

* Uzi, "Sob Story," *The Nephew Soundtrack*, 2024.

February 2, 1972

Dear God,

Last night I made a promise to give up drugs, but as usual I was weak and didn't quite make it. I think it's more in the mind than anything else. If all you do is think about dope and your lack of it, then your body will hurt. You can't lay around thinking about it, you must get out and occupy your mind.

Carole and I had a good talk. She's a beautiful person and the world would be better if there were more Caroles. I know a lot of Black men would be better off if their woman were like Carole. Black men need women who would stick by them through thick and thin. A lot of women abandon men many times for no reason at all, much less for a good reason. She is with me even after all I've done to her. I better realize where she's coming from before it's too late. It is possible for her to leave me even though she hasn't done so yet. We could have a good life and we will because I'm going to make it so.

**The ones with the dreams to get rich or die trying**
**In the slums, the fiends get a ditch and die buying**
**Goons ready to shoot—sky diving**
**A hundred I drop so please stop me if I'm lying***

But it's nothing I can't do and I'm going to do it. I can't live my life like I'm living it now because I'm really not living now at all, just existing.

I want to be able to help some young brothers and sisters. To help them avoid the hurdles I've been through lately. One of my biggest problems has been a lack of direction.

Tom is having problems with his woman. Drugs are fucking him up just like it's fucking (please excuse my language) everybody else that messes with it.

—Bob

---

* Uzi, "NASA," *The Nephew Soundtrack*, 2024.

# 19 / Lookout Boys

"Never do coke," Uzi tells me when I'm like fourteen. It never even crosses my mind to try it, but out of the blue, Uzi's adamant about it. "Never fuck with that shit."

"Okay," I tell him.

"And not even on some Nancy Reagan 'Just Say No' bullshit," he clarifies. "But on some real shit. Don't touch it. Know why?" He quizzes me. A lot of things run through my mind but I don't want to say the wrong thing.

"Why?

"Because you'll love it, Malo—that's the fuck why!" he says, deadass. This is out of nowhere. "You'll love it, little bro, and it'll destroy you and everything you love."

He goes on to tell me to "watch out" because "it's always a girl, a bad jawn with the nose candy," who introduces it. "And for girls, it's always some dude that turns them out." He says it always goes down like that. He also hips me to the racist disparity in mandatory federal sentencing laws between crack cocaine (primarily used by Blacks) and powder cocaine (primarily used by whites). Five grams of crack is five years in prison. To get five years for coke, you need five hundred grams.

> **Killers congregating at the corner store**
> **Rice and gravy, four wings, a quarter more**
> **They gave my boy a fuckin quarter in the court of law**
> **Won't touch Philly 'til he 54—he did it for a whore***

Because of that random convo with Uzi, I dip and dodge coke my whole life. And sure enough, years later, at a party in NYC, I meet a "bad jawn." She takes me into a private area and pulls out a few grams of coke. She blows two quick lines off her acrylic nails and then offers it to me. I chuckle inside at Uzi's foresight.

"I'm good," I say.

> **First came smack, then came base**
> **On attack, it's been destroying my race**
> **Whether skeletal face or a federal case**
> **From summit to plummet at an incredible pace†**

In your rhymes, Nephew, I can't help but hear all the drug references. I don't mind hearing about the weed because, as Uzi says in his letter, that's "spiritual stimuli" lol. Artists have used cannabis productively for centuries so that's not my concern, however, at the same time, it's important to be able to tap into your creativity

---

* Uzi, "Open Bar," *The Nephew Soundtrack*, 2024.
† Uzi, "NASA," *The Nephew Soundtrack*, 2024.

without relying or depending on any substances. You are the substance.

On the block, I was not in school
On them Percs, I was poppin blues*

I hear you rap about taking Percocets (oxycodone) and sipping lean (Promethazine) and it sparks memories of J Street in the nineties when the city allowed Jefferson Street (it was Jefferson Avenue in Buffalo for Bob) to become an open-air, broad-day, drug supermarket. I remember following Uzi's friends Scoop and Ted down there:

J Street looks like the "Thriller" video, all zombied out. Fiends, as thin as crack pipes, dance—the dancing dead—in the shadows and disappear then reappear somewhere else. Everything ghostly. Here—gone. Everybody's eyes curry yellow or smog gray, hopeless as sunken ships. Shit is crazy. The dealers chant inventory like a chorus: "Weed out, weed out." "Crack out, crack out." "Coke out, coke out." "Her-ron, her-ron."

When I hear you talk about doing hard drugs—"Lean in the Crush"—I pray that you do not have anything in your system that would hinder your fight for your life. I pray you are free from toxins that threaten your healing now.

He pop shit cuz his pop got hit
Then he pop a perc so he won't feel shit†

---

* Neph, "Blessings," *The Nephew Soundtrack*, 2024.
† MK Asante, "Pop of Color," *The Nephew Soundtrack*, 2024.

I hear you mention the drugs and I think about the damage to nearly everyone I grew up with. I can remember them before they became skeletons and zombies.

> **Mixin' lean with soda pop when they grievin' the kid**
> **Real dad pop up once he serve that bid**
> **Both poppin pills for the years that they whisked**
> **Tear drop tat on a face that ain't never been kissed***

I can remember Nna hiding her pills whenever certain corner boys came by. I can also remember Nna's own struggles with prescription drugs in the nineties:

Dear Carole,

I never took drugs even though they were all around me. I don't really count smoking weed as a drug but Bob was a heroin addict and my brother has been a crack addict on and off so I know drugs.

But the drugs prescribed for my depression are a different story. They serve the same purpose as crack or heroin, a way of escaping, of turning away from the pain and an excuse to leave the planet momentarily.

My drugs are legal, but the results, the high, feels the same. It doesn't make much sense to me that a doctor could know what medicine to give someone for depression anyway. Depression is so specific, so historical and so particular, how could a pill deal with all that? The pills don't deal with any of that.

All they do is make the time go by dulling my senses and making me sleep. Taking my meds is like putting a sign on my door that says "Unavailable." It works. The only person to ignore the sign is Malo. At least when he was younger, he ignored the "sign," but now as a teenager, he keeps his distance and tells other people "Mom don't feel well." Malo is staring at a woman who

---

* MK Asante, "Pop of Color," *The Nephew Soundtrack*, 2024.

doesn't seem herself. It's not that I'm not myself, but I have buried myself so that I don't feel any pain. Daudi doesn't get it and it makes him angry. Malo accepts it even if he doesn't get it. I'm in my bedroom, either in bed or in my chair, but always out of commission. I'm in a fog and I prefer it that way.

My husband believes that medicine can cure anything, I know better. He's always so encouraged every time the doctor prescribes a new medicine. "This will work" is his mantra and so off I go into another world until I tire of the charade and stop taking the medication. It isn't that the medication doesn't work but it doesn't work the way that he wants it to work. It doesn't work the way that I want it to work. He wants magic, a pill that can make me new again. But just like me, that pill doesn't exist.

God, give me strength.

—Kari

**Pure seduction, both sides, drugs and hustling**
**Is it wealth production or self-destruction?***

All my life, I watch as Uzi flirts with different drugs. When he's in Arizona, it's crystal, free base, and coke. Before he gets arrested, when he's like seventeen, he sends me a note about it:

I wish u could be out here, Malo, u should see this shit, a Philly ngh in AZ, doin rap shows, smuttin these coke-snortin Beckys and Suzzies in their $2000 a month trust fund baby condo flop houses—shit wild, just stay there for like a month partying, binging, it's nuts.

In Philly, it's Zanny bars, coke, lean, and wet. Uzi is the type to do these drugs at a party but they don't stick with him. Nna thinks he's an alcoholic and she's probably right.

---

* Uzi, "NASA," *The Nephew Soundtrack*, 2024.

However, that all changes when Uzi gets introduced to Percs. His girl Danielle gets a prescription after a car accident. Everything changes—"From summit to plummet at an incredible pace."

> Fiends chase the initial high, no aces
> Feast on the streets, prey on food, no graces
> Lost souls running loose no laces
> When they feel deserted, the high's an oasis[*]

My whole life, Uzi is consistent in his character. For instance, he's no thief. He doesn't steal and he also doesn't lie, even when it could benefit him. I remember, back in the day, Nna would be like, "Are you high?"

Uzi's like, "Yup."

He isn't money-hungry, greedy, or even entrepreneurial either. He's a pure artist. If Uzi gets money—even a little bit—he's sharing it all until he's broke. He may beg, but he will not con. He may bum, but he will not lie. However with Percs, it seems anything is possible.

> Half empty, half full, no matter when you thirsty
> Pain relieving with a Perc 30
> But it's the 30s that's really tryna hurt me[†]

The scary part is that I don't even know if the Percs Uzi's taking are actually even Percocets, because dealers cut and swap the Percs

---

[*]   Uzi, "NASA," *The Nephew Soundtrack*, 2024.
[†]   Uzi, "24 Hourz," *The Nephew Soundtrack*, 2024.

with fentanyl, which is one hundred times stronger, more addictive, and deadlier than the heroin that destroyed Bob's life.

March 9, 1972

Dear God,

We're watching *All in the Family* and Roger's over here. We're all high now because when Roger came over he stayed for a few minutes and then he went to meet his people and get his package.

I've been talking to Carole lately and the story is that Tina (who acts as an accountant for the Black Dance Workshop) noticed a difference between her figures and the figures from the bank statement. So she took her books to the bank and since the bank had all the checks I wrote it wasn't easy for them to first see a lot of checks were written to me and second that Carole's signature wasn't her signature at all. I've had a talk with a bank official because the legal department got in touch with Carole and explained the situation to her and then she relayed all the information to me. They want all the money back from me in May or they will prosecute me for forgery. The total amount of the checks I wrote is $1,250. That's a lot of money.

Another hassle is that the funds involved were federal, which puts things in another light.

> Pure seduction, both sides, drugs and hustling
> Is it wealth production or self-destruction?
> Feds build cases with stealth construction
> And heads left for the rush of inhaled combustion*

But to make things harder than they are, this afternoon after waiting for a ride to the school, I went to the gym to do my thief thing. Pickings were

---

*   Uzi, "NASA," *The Nephew Soundtrack*, 2024.

slim at first with all my earnings amounting to $7.22, all in change. But I had made up my mind to get over regardless of what it took . . . and it did take me doing some jive actions, to make a long story short. I had to take somebody's bag, run out into the hall, take out the person's wallet from the bag. After taking the wallet, I ran down to the basement, out a locked door and up to Main Street, hitched a ride to Amherst Street.

I long for the day when I wake up in the morning feeling alright and secure in the knowledge that I won't have to get some dope sometime during the day in order to feel alright. Knowing that if I don't get some drugs that my body will feel alright, when I kicked a cold around last Thanksgiving time. It was a good feeling not having to get drugs, knowing that I could go to sleep early if I wanted to without my body acting up. I would like to experience that feeling again, but I won't be able to unless I kick, and maybe kicking a cold would be the best way.

Smoking and being high enough to nod. I nod every day, and one of these days I'm going to wake up and see myself engulfed in a ring of flames burning up.

So many times, I've caught myself dropping my cigarette onto my neck when I couldn't catch it.

I'm nodding right now, so I have to be careful.

—Bob

# 20 / The Blues

Uzi's character changes completely when he starts popping Percs. As if he's shape-shifting, I see him morph into an addict, morph into an "astronaut man," "'bout to go to outta space" like his pops.

OG, Philly Blunts, OE, J Street,
Body over bottles with that purple yellow codeine*

Before he even gets addicted to Percs, Uzi breaks it down for me, how a lot of people end up shooting up heroin from Percs.

"It's a natural, unnatural evolution," he says. "They're both opioids, heroin comes from plants and Percs are synthetic, but they're both in the opioid family and do the same thing," he explains. "After a while, them Perc 30s, they call 'em 'blues,' get expensive. That's when someone tells you like, 'you payin' all that money for the Percs when you can get like three stamp bags of heron.' Next thing you know, a mothfucka is like this," Uzi taps his veins. "Shootin' that shit up . . . Ain't no coming back after that."

---

* Uzi, "Sob Story," *The Nephew Soundtrack*, 2024.

> Come out the wood works airbrushed on a hood shirt
> My bro was with me til he got hooked on them good Percs*

Nna calls me—I can hear the worry in her soft voice—to tell me she sees a change in Uzi's behavior.

"Daudi calls at night and he sounds crazed out of his mind. He begs me to save him."

"Save?" I ask to be sure because that doesn't sound like him.

"Yes, he uses the word 'save'! I am sure he was crying and high! I didn't get one letter while he was in jail. Only demands. I'm afraid that he's already like, sort of, given up."

"He hasn't given up," I assure her.

"You can't give up at only thirty-four years old. What's ahead of you? You can't just live off other people. It just breaks my heart. Anyway, that's life. I don't know if he has to wear an iron bracelet. He does have a backyard and the weather's okay. I sent him some money, a number of books. You have to be grateful for whatever you have. In his case, he has a beautiful brand-new baby boy."

When Nna talks like this, I just listen. It's hard to hear, to process, and my instinct is to defend my brother.

"Danielle calls to say she doesn't have food. He doesn't understand. I'm just tired. I wasn't going to offer to pick him up from jail. I went to

---

*   MK Asante, "Mudcloth," *The Nephew Soundtrack*, 2024.

Arizona to get him from prison. I wanted him to come out of jail and say, 'whatever it takes, I'll man up and take care of my family.' I'm not saying that he didn't get a bad break, but thousands of people have had it worse. He's thirty-four; this happened when he was seventeen. As Obama says, it can't happen without trying," Nna says. I smile because Nna loves her some Obama, always finding a way to slip him in.

She plays me a voice mail from Uzi.

"Yeah, Mom, this Daahoud, heard Danielle just called you and all that. What can I say? I left you with like a twenty-minute message like three weeks ago—did you ever call me back? No. And Y'all wonder why I don't mess with my family—cause y'all never got my back. A mother would call her son when a dude needs help . . . Spill his guts and be pleading for help like that, you think you called me, did you call me, no you didn't, you didn't, that's what you been doing all my life . . ." Words slurry—I can hear the Percs trampling over his meter like a stalking horse.

> Damn, look what the system did to you
> Long gats and face tats at an interview
> Nghs taking this entertainment too literal
> Hooked on pills, man, they chained to the chemical*

He goes on—

". . . All the fuckin hate I got in my heart is because of you. I never did nothing to you. All I did was fucking be born. All y'all

---

* Uzi, "Open Bar," *The Nephew Soundtrack*, 2024.

did was fuckin' pamper Malo and reject me, even in times of need
when I call you and spill my guts to you . . . You don't even call me
back. I'm your son, your firstborn. All you can do is tell her—her
of all people!—we dealing with some hood-rat nastiness, tell her
'he can't come here.' Well, you know what, you can't come here!
You can't come into my heart! You dig what I'm saying? I don't care
if you disown me, I don't give a fuck . . ."

Uzi's words shock Nna on a few levels. She can also tell that he's
"high on something," as she puts it.

"I feel like deep down inside, he's given up. Self-hatred makes you
vicious. To lash out at his mother, at his girlfriend. I don't want him
to lash out against the baby, because then you bring another human
being into the cycle. And what it's doing to me—he'll never know."

***

Nna can't stand hypocrisy and I think that's the part that gets
her riled up the most. "Here he is with a teenage son who he's never
even said two words to," she whips. "Hasn't lifted a finger to help
his son and wants to whine about his family not having his back,
after all we've done for him? The nerve!"

I notice the change in Uzi too. Not just his words, but he starts
hitting me up for money daily. First fives and tens, then twenties
and hundreds—says it's to buy clothes for a job interview, or bus
fare for a job interview, or food for the baby; it's never enough. This
isn't his MO. He's my brother, so I can feel when something is off.
The moment I say "No" to his money request, all hell breaks loose.
He snaps on me like he did on Nna.

Nna says, "In my heart, I fear that he is heading towards 'death'! . . . I pray that I am wrong and instead it is the 'death' of the lifestyle that he is leading now."

April 20, 1972

Dear God,

I'm not going to rap too long tonight because I have some business to take care of later on this morning, so I want to get a little sleep. I've already put myself in a bad position now by missing appointments when all I have to do is get my lazy behind out of the bed. I know the appointments are important. They are the difference between going to jail and not going. Ain't that important enough? I hope it's not too late. If it is, I'll have to resign myself to the fact that I'm going to jail. Maybe I need to go, it'll take me off the streets and give me some time to think things out. I'm supposedly man enough to dig the hole but not man enough to climb out of it.

**Man those haters they be nosey as binoculars**
**Feds say we a ring, so the DA got a mop for us***

Now I'm running scared again. I broke into Carole's house Sunday night. Went through the broken basement window to the back of the house, up through the basement door, which I had broken open the last time I went over there and into the house. I knew I had a good idea that the receipts from Saturday night's concert were at her apartment somewhere and just as I was about to give up looking . . . I find it. On the desk we had in the apartment on Dewey Street. I took $220, which $90 I blew on dope, paid Chucky the $10. I'm doing so wrong. I can't even face any of the Workshop anymore. They know what I've been doing.

—Bob

---

* Uzi, "Yada," *The Nephew Soundtrack*, 2024.

# 21 / Swan Song

The unthinkable.

Danielle decides to send Uzi's suicide letter to Nna, who tearfully sends it to me.

To Mom and Malo: Fuck you.

To Fukai and Nasir: Sorry I couldn't be the father I wanted to be.

To Danielle: Rot in hell. Fuck you bitch.

—Uzi

# 22 / For Brown Girls

Uzi's swan song stirs my mind back to the 1990s when I read what Nna wrote in her journal about suicide:

*There are moments when I can function but the point is I don't want to function. I want no part of this life. The pills aid my escape. Sometimes I take more than I'm supposed to.*

*No one knows what I'm taking, just the doctor. I keep stockpiles, always making allowances for that day when I might need to permanently "leave." "Leaving" has been on my mind most of my life. My first attempt at suicide was at twelve. I tried to overdose on aspirin. I was eighteen when I tried again. I took an overdose of pills. I was hospitalized. I didn't tell my family. So now I have my stash just in case I need to permanently check out.*

*The escape I yearn for is real. I want to escape the harsh upbringing of my childhood and a mother who blamed me for our poverty. I want to escape a husband who promised to take care of me and instead I was taking care of him. I want to escape a world that seemed to have broken every promise made in my dreams.*

I watch Nna struggle to overcome this—through therapy, self-care, diet, family, and dance—and now her will to live is stronger than ever.

She says, "When I am not in the throes of work, it can get awfully quiet but in my head, it is quite noisy, but I have a passion for life and want to live very much. There is a stereotype that artists are more prone to depression than the rest of the population. I don't know if that is true but I do know that as a woman of color, who was sexually traumatized as a child, was made to feel as though it was my fault, I have suffered from depression since I was a young teenager. I have tried to commit suicide three times and have been hospitalized twice." Her words are heavy but necessary. I love her openness and willingness to put it out there.

Nna hears my silence, not sure how to respond.

"I do the same thing," she affirms. "My silence is my retreat from the world and a haven at times and I guess I passed it on to you."

"Yeah, just processing, Mom. You are so strong. I wish these things were talked about more," I say, thinking about the stigma attached to it all.

"The Black community doesn't handle depression well," she quips. "We ignore it, are ashamed, and wonder why we don't just get over 'it,' not knowing that the 'it' is plural. People still talk about depression in hushed tones. When I was a child, they used expressions like 'they had to put him away' and 'he is in the sanatorium.' Despite our technological advances, society hasn't yet come to grips with depression. It is in spite of all of this and more that I have managed to do all that I have done. And yet it isn't enough. As an older woman now, who has suffered life's battering and also experienced life's wonderful generosity, I continue to struggle with my demons."

Uzi's outro suicide note is a striker-fired trigger, bringing my mind to reflect on my life, mental health, and my village. I can't stop thinking about Kwame and Karyn.

I see the caramel cheekbones of little Kwame, his baby dreads peaking under his black Phillies hat. Kwame is the son of Nna's friend Ms. Yhema. We grow up together—playing ball, slapboxing, getting hook parts in our haircuts—and Kwame's sister, Dina, was my first love. Nna named him "Kwame" at birth, and when Kwame's son was born, Kwame names him . . . Nasir! It's hard for me and Nna to grapple with the grenade that is Kwame's suicide.

I see the radiance of my dear friend Karyn Washington, founder of For Brown Girls, a movement she starts to inspire women and fight colorism. She also launches the #darkskinredlip project after a comment by rapper A$AP Rocky about red lips and dark girls not mixing.

A wonder woman of the world, Karyn's energy is Victoria Falls, her intelligence, the Lighthouse of Alexandria, and her endless beauty, the Nile River. I remember her breaking it down for me at the Bromo Seltzer Arts Tower in Baltimore:

"Until starting this movement, I struggled. But soon into my journey, I quickly found an abundance of myself in others, in Black women who inspired me and in those who loved me, who had been there with me all along." She speaks with a passion and eloquence that honors her ideas.

This is for brown girls when the rainbow ain't enough
Searching for love, but all they want is lust

Don't let them build you up to tear you down
Don't let them kill your joy or steal your smile*

She continues, "Through my journey, I also learned that victims of colorism have many identities; different personalities, have different faces, and live in different places. I connected with girls all over the US and across the world. Some girls got so much hate from their family members that they were nearly to the point of suicide."

This is in your memory, still feel your energy
Still remember that day I felt like the enemy
Then you ended it all and it felt like the end of me
Late nights in the studio bring back sweet memory
Of your essence, knowing you was a blessing†

"We were all sisters: girls from India, to Canada, to New York, to London. Girls and women of not only African descent (which was what I was mainly focusing on—colorism in the Black community geared specifically towards those with darker hues) but Indian, Hispanic, and Asian, as well face-color discrimination. Their stories were captivating to me."

Apologies to the universe for neglection
Ms. Washington, the capitol of lessons‡

"I felt that there was a deeper connection to be made between all of us who had struggled with accepting our shade of skin. We had all felt or been told at some point in our lives that our skin was too

---

*†‡ MK Asante, "FBG," *The Nephew Soundtrack*, 2024.

dark. It seemed to be universally accepted that lighter was right, and we were, in our existence, tragically flawed."

Karyn, mourning the loss of her mother and unable to find the support she needed, including, sadly, from me, took her life on April 8, 2014, at twenty-two years old.

> For Brown Girls when the rainbow ain't visible
> When life coming at you, world cold miserable
> So critical we gotta see your vision through
> Black girl magic the universe in need of you
> Black girl tragic close my eyes all I see is you
> Rest in Power, For Brown Girls we gonna see it through*

May 7, 1972

Dear God,

All of my energy and every thought goes into one thing now and that's getting high. Seems like nothing else matters to me. Just so I can have that dope, I'll do anything, lie, cheat, steal, implicate others, normally Carole, into my wrongdoings. In my opinion, that's wrong. I need money to try methadone to help me kick.

> Block is hot, cops making sure cells-see-us
> Freeze Kelvin, hot ones, now they melting
> You bitches gonna learn today, welcome to Spelman
> Scarlet letter on your back when you a felon†

---

* MK Asante, "FBG," *The Nephew Soundtrack*, 2024.
† Uzi, "24 Hourz," *The Nephew Soundtrack*, 2024.

Slowly but surely I'm realizing that I had a lot going for me. Especially last summer when I had that job with Model Cities making $200 a week. Could have made a lot of contacts with that job. I had a good basketball game, which is not the case now because I don't play a lot now, so my game is off, my body isn't finely tuned anymore.

—Bob

# 23 / Killing & the Coke

I go to Nna's house when I get the suicide note.

"A mighty storm has come our way and I am trying to make sense of it all," Nna says as soon as she sees me. "Your brother is alive, he's in the hospital. A sense of relief rushes through me. "He broke his neck trying to hang himself."

"I'm glad he's alive," I say. "Opioid addiction leads to people being very susceptible to suicide."

"I know, I know." She looks at me the way she does when trauma explodes in our laps. "We're in crisis."

"Spiritual crisis."

Uzi is predisposed to heroin because of Bob's heroin use. Half of someone's susceptibility to drug addiction is linked to genetics. When Uzi tells me not to do coke because I'll love it, he knows not to do heroin because he's predisposed to love it. He is born addicted to it and must avoid it at all costs. Like you, Nephew. Avoid it like the plague.

Just like Uzi tells me back in the day, I'm telling you now, don't do it—the lean, the Percs, coke, etc.—and don't promote it to the young bucks. That's vital to your recovery and survival.

> **If you feelin what I spoke**
> **And got some feeling and some hope**
> **What I'm revealing in my quote**
> **We stop the killing and the coke***

As you see from Bob's letters to God, heroin is something Bob struggled with mightily. He didn't want to be an addict and was aware of the damage it was doing in his young life. One of the things that lunges off the page at me is when Bob says, "The most important thing is that I replace drugs with something else. Replace the artificial high of drugs with the natural high of life."

Bob's recognition is key. And this is where music comes in.

Your brain comes with a built-in opioid system, which, when triggered, releases endorphins. Endorphins are your body's natural painkillers and opioids like Percs just mimic endorphins. The endorphins give a feeling of pleasure, a high, a pain relief that is healthy for you, for the world. Making music triggers endorphins.

Let your music be the "something else" that Bob isn't able to find. We all need a "something else."

---

\* Uzi, "Sob Story," *The Nephew Soundtrack*, 2024.

Name-less-ness due to aim-less-ness
But give em' purpose & watch the language shift*

For me, that "something else" is the Blank Page.

*The blank page begs me to tell a story—dares me to tell one—one that's never been told before, and to tell it like it will never be told again. The blank page lights up a room in my heart that I didn't know existed . . .*

*I stare at the blank page, an ocean of white alive with possibility. I hear myself take a breath, then exhale—deep, like I just rose from underwater . . .*

*My hand shaking, trembling like it's freezing. Then it hits: a silence louder than all the music I've ever heard in my life. All the light in the world, in one beam, before me. I start writing and don't stop . . .*

Even though the suicide note was drug-related, Uzi's apology to you for not being the father "he wanted to be" is a big step for Uzi. Up until then, I never hear him express any accountability or regret.

Uzi's suicide note is rock bottom and sometimes that's what we need. When Bob goes to jail, Nna's mom writes him and says "Maybe jail is the best place for you."

With Uzi, we use his near-death moment to cement our love, to affirm our commitment, to help him get clean from the Percs and get back to himself. "I am my brother's keeper" resonates.

---

* MK Asante, "Mudcloth," *The Nephew Soundtrack*, 2024.

There's a story in the 1918 book *The Higher Powers of Mind and Spirit* by Ralph Waldo Trine about a little girl carrying a big baby boy on her back.

"Do you know that incident in connection with the little Scottish girl? She was trudging along, carrying as best she could a boy younger, but it seemed almost as big as she herself, when one remarked to her how heavy he must be for her to carry, when instantly came the reply: 'He's na heavy. He's mi brother.'"

That's how I feel about Uzi: "He ain't heavy, he's my brother."

"It's never too late," is still my refrain, belief, and way of life.

Nna writes him a special letter on his birthday, honoring and challenging her "firstborn son."

02/02/2014

Dear Daahoud,

What do you do when you have done all you can and it seems like it is not enough? You must stand! My firstborn son, you must not give up! Hold on, take one step and angels will rush in to assist you. Don't look at the past and judge yourself. We all have pasts and if we let the past haunt us, we can never go forward. Tomorrow is not promised but it is tomorrow that you must look to. Your heart can only break once, now is the time to rebuild. You are not alone. You have family and friends who dearly love you. Life is full of challenges for all of us.

No one escapes the vicissitudes of life.

On this day of your birth, remember that your mother asked God that if he had to choose, he must give you life. I carried and loved you knowing that our lives were at risk. I trusted, prayed, and finally let go so that you could live. Please put yourself in your mother's place, knowing that I have made many mistakes, but I take heart that I made the right decision in having you. You and your brother, Khumalo, are the best things in my life.

My love for you has no borders, boundaries, and it never abates. I am your mother. Every morning I say your name and every night before my eyes close, I say it again. I pray for strength and courage, and I ask that you receive the ancestor's blessing in taking the next step. You are not alone!

I am your mother, the woman who gave you life. I am your mother, the woman who had to be cut open so that you could live. I am your mother, hear me, feel me, and gather your inner resources and just take one step. You will look up and others will be coming towards you. You are not alone!

On this day of your birth, take heart, you are not alone and you have most of your life ahead of you. On this day of your birth, you are not alone. Don't ever forget that.

Love,

Your mother

***

June 4, 1972

Dear God,

I'm always scared, scared to do this, scared to do that. I'm scared to undergo being withdrawn from dope (heroin). When will I put aside my fear and take a step forward. I've been standing around for a long time. I really shouldn't be in the situation I'm in, no home of my own, no job, no plans, ambitions, future (the way things are now).

**Michelin chef grind, I better make it**
**Might been missing my shine cause I hesitated***

---

* Uzi, "24 Hourz," *The Nephew Soundtrack*, 2024.

One thing I would say is that I'm not enjoying life at all. I get up in the morning really only thinking of dope. If I get over I just sit around Tom's house looking at TV, then go looking to get over again. I'm scared to go out for fear of running into the police who might be looking for me for various reasons. Nothing to look forward to, I'm never with Carole anymore. I haven't made love in a long while. My penis is a nonfunctional part of my body now because of drugs. I'm just existing not living, not enjoying life just nodding and existing. I'm wasting my life away slowly but surely.

—Bob

# 24 / Bombs over Badlands

I'm thankful for Uzi's second chance.

"It's not your time, bro. You still have work to do," I say to him when he's laid up at Jefferson Frankford Hospital in Kensington.

His Perc-induced suicide note and "fuck you" to us are unsuccessful in pushing us away. Words, especially words we know he doesn't mean, aren't enough to stop the flow of love that bum-rushes him. I read somewhere that "your heart is a polished mirror that you have to wipe clean of the veil of dust (and blood) that has gathered upon it, because it is destined to reflect the light." This is Uzi's "wipe clean."

I see the shock in his face when he sees my face at the hospital door. I cock my head animatedly like Loc Dog in *Don't Be a Menace*.

"What?" I say, slow-stepping into the room, nodding my head to an imaginary beat, "*Woooowooooowooooo.*" "What, y'all thought y'all wasn't gonna see me?" Uzi busts out laughing at the Ol' Dirty Bastard reference, which makes me keep going. "I'm the Osiris of this shit Wu-Tang is here forever, motherfuckers . . . I'ma rub your ass in the moonshine, Let's take it back to 'seventy-nine . . ." I pass the imaginary microphone to Uzi and he falls right in.

"I bomb atomically," Uzi lights up . . . and then I join him and together we rap "Triumph":

". . . Socrates's philosophies and hypotheses . . . Can't define how I be dropping these mockeries . . ."

We embrace for like ten minutes, a sweaty, hairy, big-ass bear hug.

"You know that Triumph sample is from this Detroit Gospel group called the Rance Allen Group?"

"I didn't even know it was a sample," I say.

"Everything's a sample. The original song is called 'Just Found Me.' Check it out." I think about how the sample is used in hip-hop, in life, to honor the best of the past to create something new. I think about how Uzi samples Bob and how you sample both of them.

"My bad bro," he says, looking around the room.

"Stop that," I say, admiring the sharp contours of his profile.

"Love you, bro," he tells me.

"Ditto, big bro, ditto," I say like Patrick Swayze in *Ghost*. I remember watching *Ghost* with Uzi and being shook. I'll never forget what the Subway Ghost says: "You take all your emotions! All your pain, all your love, all your passion, all your rage! Just push it all the way down into the pit of your stomach! And then let it explode, like a reactor!"

Locked down for being brown and denied appeal
But watch him come home set, look what time reveal
Look what they ain't kill, what slave ships can't steal
I lane-shift in a spaceship that's on four wheels*

"And it's still not too late to be that father you said you wanted to be," I say.

"C'mon man," he says, like he doesn't buy it.

"It's not. You know my friend Jon?"

"Light skin, curly-top, baseball-playin' Jon from South Philly?"

"Yup, he's been one of my best friends forever." I remind Uzi that when Jon was growing up—all through elementary, middle, and high school—Jon's dad wasn't in his life.

"Yo, they actually walked right past each other on the street and neither of them knew."

I tell Uzi that Jon and his dad didn't reconnect until Jon was about seventeen. And that now Jon—a dedicated father and a husband—drives every week from central Jersey to his second home: his dad's barbershop on Fifty-Seventh Street in West Philly.

---

* MK Asante, "Mudcloth," *The Nephew Soundtrack*, 2024.

Uzi's eyes spell intrigue. He nods his head in affirmation and asks, "What's his barbershop called?"

"It's called Cutz to the T—lil' play on words there because his dad's name is Timothy—and Jon won't let any other barber touch his hair."

I tell Uzi that Jon always celebrates his mom for not bad-talking or interfering with Tim's ability to father. Since Uzi doesn't really know your mom, I explain to him how your mom is the same way.

"Jon's mom, Nasir's mom, our mom, these are real amazing women who, despite it all, put their children's best interest first!" I show Uzi a picture of Jon and Tim in the barbershop. "At this point, his dad has been present in his life for more years than he wasn't. Can't change the past, but they changed their present and future."

The inside of Cutz to the T is beautiful and reminds me of a Black men's wellness center. There are baby and graduation photos tucked in the corners of mirrors, a screen print painting of the iconic Buffalo Soldiers, a black-and-white picture of Muhammad Ali shaking hands with Elijah Muhammad, and various photos of Jon's dad in the shop with celebrities in his barber chair: a young, Sixers-era Charles Barkley with the backslash part in his hair; Denzel Washington, Just Leon.

"Think about where they started, Uzi, and look at where they are now!" I point out. "Just the other day Jon told me that his dad's shop is his safe haven."

"They bond in that chair," Uzi says.

"Exactly."

Uzi nods righteously, "That's thorough."

A few weeks later, Nna calls me with a rush of energy.

"You won't believe what happened today," Nna tells me on the phone.

"Is everything okay?" I say, anticipating bad news.

"Great! Daahoud came and he brought Fukai with him," she says. Her enthusiasm is contagious.

"He brought Fukito?" I light up.

"Yes! Fukai adores his father and Daahoud adores his son. Daahoud came in with a six-pack of tall beer, which he preceded to drink in the two hours that he was at my house. Still, I was happy to see him, and he wasn't high on drugs!"

"Beautiful."

"I did something that I have never done before. I brought down the photo albums, including one that I had organized to give to Daahoud one day. It was an amazing experience for me and for Daahoud. There were pictures of Daahoud when he was a little baby and all through his youth. All of the houses that we lived in over the years. Daahoud seemed to delight in the memory of all of them."

As Nna talks, I can picture them, with the old pictures, creating new pictures.

"Memory as informant."

The next part of Uzi's journey is wildfire.

A huge blaze breaks out on Uzi's block, on Pearl Street. It's a raging inferno across the street from his house. I feel like fire is familiar in Philly.

> When I iterate, how I incinerate,
> I'm fire, only know how to speak in hundred centigrade
> Son is a heatwave no commiserate
> Weight of my words keep my pen in shape[*]

"We moved into a burning city," Uzi always says when he talks about first moving to Philly in the eighties. "And it's still on fucking fire." He nods.

> If you a cop on the beat then you can beat a body
> The force said they using force, but it's just a homi[†]

Uzi's talking about the MOVE Bombing. Around the time we move to Philly, in 'eighty-five, the Philadelphia Police Department—under the direction of Mayor Wilson Goode—drops two C4 bombs on a Black back-to-nature organization called

---

[*]  Uzi, "Yada," *The Nephew Soundtrack*, 2024.
[†]  Uzi, "Open Bar," *The Nephew Soundtrack*, 2024.

MOVE. Eleven MOVE members, including women and kids, are
killed in the destruction.

> Sleuths on the roof putting the noose to the grindin'
> We Mayor Goode, you MOVE and we bombin'*

One of the two survivors, Ramona Africa, becomes close with Nna.
Nna choreographs a dance and writes the poem, "Raaaahmonaaaah!"
in her honor. Seven dancers in white, two in black, fill the space. Drums
roll. Slides of the fire in the background. Locs. Gazes. Anger.

Child of Isis and Osiris
Ebony doe-eyed woman
Wrapped in your locs
Dreading the fire yesterday
Ramonaaaaah!

Locked in a steel castle
Where is your King?
Ramona Mona Bo Bona Ramona! Fee Fi Mo Mona Ramona!

Miss Lady Woman
Cast your hair toward Africa
And weave net to
Swing Low and Carry You Home!
Ramona! Ramona!

MOVE, Ramona!
And as you sway, we'll move with you

---

\* MK Asante x Uzi, "Bangers (Remix)," *The Nephew Soundtrack*, 2024.

No fire can drown out your light
No flame can dim your glow
You are cowries, serpentine, malacyte
You are Ramona!

You are Malacyte, Cowry, Serpentine
You are Ramona!
Reflections of Nzinga lying the cut to set your people free
Ramona Mona Bo Bona Ramona! Fee Fi Mo Mona Ramona!"
Ramona! Ramona!
Raaaahmonaaaah!

***

July 3, 1972

Dear God,

    I get sentenced Thursday the 18th of this month!

**Nothing changed since we came off the ships scarred**
**The plan is to put you in the cell we the SIM card***

    I get sentenced Thursday and I'm anticipating going to the pen for 3 months.

    —Bob

---

*   Uzi, "Open Bar," *The Nephew Soundtrack*, 2024.

# 25 / Fire on Pearl Street

There's something magical about Uzi. He's the only person I know that studies magic. His thing is misdirection, card tricks, and of course, disappearing acts. He says, "magic is all about misdirection. Large movements to cover small movements."

Which brings me back to the fire on Uzi's block, Pearl Street.

Uzi runs into the burning house to save an old man. It makes the same Action News TV that the shooting does.

"A neighbor pulled the elderly man, they call Pops, from his burning home on the 200 block of Pearl Street in Norristown, not far from a firehouse," the anchor on TV says.

"The neighbor, identified as Daahoud Asante, heard the man screaming for help from his second-floor bedroom, where he had been sleeping when the fire started. Asante and the victim's son raced toward the home. They opened the door and encountered smoke pouring down the stairway. Asante tells Action News that's when they made the decision to rush up the smoke-filled stairway. They freed the man from the bedroom."

What?! I watch in awe, my mouth stuck open like I'm at the dentist.

They show Uzi on TV and my eyes Velcro to the screen. This is the Uzi I remember looking up to. He looks clear-eyed and strong.

"We grabbed him. I pulled him down the steps."

"This guy!" I say, chuckling in disbelief that Uzi's on the News.

A sweaty Uzi continues on TV, "After that, everything was on fire." The anchor says, "Pops was rushed to Temple Hospital to be treated for smoke inhalation. His condition has not been released . . . Asante does not want to be called a hero. He said he just did what he hopes any person would do when they see someone in need of help."

This is major for Uzi, for the family, and of course for the man the neighborhood calls Pops. I can't help but think of his pops, Bob, and how maybe Uzi wishes he could have saved him. And maybe Uzi did save Bob, by saving Pops and giving you a glimpse into his true spirit.

"It's never too late," I tell Uzi like a broken record.

Bob's letters to God stop when he goes to jail. But I think they are beautifully instructive for us as they relate to the power of addiction, the urgent wisdom of avoidance, and the necessity of believing in yourself. When Bob goes to jail, he sends Nna one more letter.

But before he sends Nna the letter, your great grandmother Ruth reaches out to him. She gets little envelopes that have the "The Truth from Ruth" printed across the bottom:

June 5, 1972

Dear Bob,

I am sorry to hear of your bad luck but can't help feeling that jail could be your lucky break.

I am writing this letter to you because there is a time in everyone's life, even though we are grown up, when we wish our mother was there to talk to, to have the feeling that someone is in our corner.

I was fortunate to have mom until I was 20 years old, but there have been times since when I wished she was there to talk to.

Now that you are physically withdrawn from drug usage, why not make a new plan to become emotionally withdrawn from drug usage.

I am sure you realize that anything worthwhile that is achieved is accomplished after having decided a definite goal, either planning how to arrive at that goal or taking the first step toward that goal of contributing, one step at a time.

For instance, if you've decided that drugs are no longer for you, then it is important that upon leaving jail, you get a job. Try not to get hung up on what kind of work you are or aren't willing to do or whether the job is prestigious, etc. The main thing is that you get a job that will provide you with the essentials, then stay away from your old buddies and old hangouts. And stay away from the University until you are sure that your habit is a thing of the past.

When I met you, I was impressed with you. I said to myself, what a fine boyfriend Carole has. Don't prove me wrong. You are a fine young man.

Try not to let self-doubt and self-destruction feelings get the better of you. Unfortunately, these feelings are something we must all contend with.

My grandfather used to call it the devil. He used to say, don't let the devil win.

So, chin up, Bob, and don't let the devil win.

Mom, Ruth

(Carole's mother)

June 19, 1972

Dear Carole,

I was just lying in bed in my cell reading a copy of *Black Enterprise* when I thought about you. Really, I was thinking about your being on TV last Saturday and doing your solo "My man is gone." I know that you were communicating with me and since I had told all of the brothers in the gallery (the section of cells I'm on) they sort of felt the same way. The dance evoked two different emotions within me. First of all, pride that you're mine and that you're beautiful and secondly a sense of personal shame because of my own situation.

Being here on a dope charge when I have a beautiful and black woman such as you. Let me tell you the brothers really dug it. Whenever they see women on TV they scream and holler, even when it's white women such as the Golddiggers. But I could sense a deeper feeling of appreciation on their part while you were on. Everyone was asking who's that? Who's that? Tell so and so someone in here is in love with them. Everybody except you that is because I made it known that you're mine. One cat said, "Bob, I don't know if you can keep her," with my being in here and you know though I think about who's trying to rap to you since I've been here, I believe in us. I believe in your love for me, which you've showed me time and time again, my love for you.

I beg you for forgiveness for all I've done to make you sad and unhappy.

Drugs are no longer a part of my life. I've been debating should I even smoke reefer anymore. Hopefully by the time I get out I won't even be smoking cigarettes.

I was so proud of you Saturday. Dancing to me, rapping about the BDW program.

Did you know that your mother wrote me? She said some beautiful things and gave me some instructions on how to get myself together, which I'm going to follow.

—Bob

# 26 / The Sacred Toolbox

In the last text message that Nipsey Hussle writes to his mom, he says, "I'm grateful. I have a studio again. I'm just happy and ready to work."

Nna loves being in the dance studio. As a kid I travel with her around Philly to teach dance at different studios. I remember those days in the studio—Nna's waist wrapped in African cloth, leotards beneath, her salt-and-pepper hair pulled into a perfect bun—watching her teach the Umfundalai technique at Freedom Theater, PHILADANCO!, University of the Arts, Swarthmore, and Temple.

**Before this rap shit stacked a couple hundred G's**
**Asanti's on the bulletproof in 2003[*]**

Nna says, "When I'm in the studio, I feel empowered. When I'm in the studio, I'm creating my world."

The studio—"The stu" as you call it—is a sacred toolbox in our family.

---

[*] Privaledge featuring Nipsey Hussle, "So Cold," *Joe World*, 2012.

I remember your first time in the studio, Nephew, like watching Clark Kent go into the phone booth and come out Superman— "Up, up, and away!"

I also remember Uzi's first time in the studio, like watching Bruce Banner get zapped by the Gammasphere and transform into the Hulk with unstoppable rage—"Hulk smash!"

You and your pops, though you've never met, both record at the same studio, Wonderful Sound Studios in Chapel Hill. You both pour your souls into the same Neuman U87 microphone. Your voices share compression through the same Tube-Tech. Your spirits occupy the same space, separated by time.

I name Wonderful Sound Studios after my son Wonderful Legacy Asante, who passed away in 2014 from anencephaly. Anencephaly is a serious condition, a birth defect that is fatal 100 percent of the time. Most babies with anencephaly are stillborn. They tell us Wonderful will be stillborn or, at most, will live for two to three hours.

Halfway into the pregnancy, when we find out his condition, I name him Wonderful.

"You can't say Wonderful and be sad" is my logic. We didn't want his name to conjure grief or despair, but rather joy and love. Wonderful's death is imminent, but his life is imminent too, regardless of the span. We didn't want his name to evoke sadness or despair. Life is a gift, as Grandma Beverly, Bob, and Nna say, and none of us know for how long we will be here, so his life is Wonderful.

Also, in Zimbabwe, people commonly name their children Bigboy, Kisswell, Thanksalot, Godknows, Temptation, Shopman,

Brain, Confidence, Decent, Pardon, Blessings, Innocence, Endless, and Future.

Like Wonderful's existence, being an uncle to you, Nasir, makes me realize the gift of life, of each precious moment. Life, no matter how long, is worth living and being celebrated.

The doctors say he will not survive birth. They say even if he survives birth, he'll never be able to breathe without a machine. They say even if he survives birth and takes a breath, he will only have a few breaths.

But the doctors are not Wonderful. They do not know Wonderful. Just like the doctors didn't know Grandma Beverly would defeat her cancer forty years ago and raise her children. Just like the doctors now don't know how strong you are, Nephew.

They say Wonderful will not survive birth, but he does. Not only does he survive, he parties with us for three days before eventually passing away in my arms. I learned a lifetime in those three days.

I dedicate the soundtrack for my memoir *Buck* to Wonderful, who passed during the recording:

> *This soundtrack is dedicated to my son Wonderful Legacy Asante, who passed away during the recording of this soundtrack.*
>    *Wonderful Legacy Asante, October 31, 2014–November 2, 2014.*
>    *I named him Wonderful because you can't say wonderful and be sad, you can't say "wonderful" and be down and depressed, nahmean. It's a blessing. No matter how long you're here for, it's a blessing.*

*He taught me so much, though; in only a short amount of time, he taught me so many things.*

*He taught me to maximize each moment. He taught me that you can live a lifetime in a weekend. He taught me that everything is a miracle, everybody is fragile. The fact that you're here right now, the fact that you're listening to this right now, you're a miracle, it's a miracle. It's not guaranteed.*

*He taught me to fear nothing, not even death. He told me that as he passed away on my chest. I took my shirt off, he had anencephaly, so his brain was right against my chest. And he told me that. He spoke to me. He told me that love conquers everything. Much love to his mom Maya, much love to Aion.*

Later, when I learn about Bodhisattva Wonderful Sound, I decide to build a music and post-production studio and name it Wonderful Sound Studios. It's yours, Nephew, designed with you in mind, so that you may always have a place to exercise your voice.

Wonderful Sound, according to the Buddha's account in the *Lotus Sutra*, "is a composer and musician who can play hundreds of instruments and served the Buddha, Dharma, and Sangha with his music. Wonderful Sound has the ability to understand all living beings at a very deep level by understanding the mental situation and inner expression of everyone, their deep longings, their suffering, their desires, and their dreams."

# 27 / Flowers

I'm sleeping in my little nook of the hospital lobby, tinted sunglasses over my eyes, when I hear screams and shrieks. I squeeze my closed eyes even tighter and wince. I don't want to wake up. I don't want to face the screams.

**Ain't too many endings**
**It's either the box or the prison**[*]

I remember us playing basketball at the park around the corner from Great-Grandma Ruth's house in the Bronx. I see your young-buck crossover and step back. I remember watching you blow glass at the Crefeld School—Iron Man face mask on, gripping hot metal—and the vase you made Nna for her favorite kind of flower: bird-of-paradise. I remember us in Redondo Beach in Cali watching the sea lions for hours. I remember the drums in your grandma's church and how you mesmerized the pews.

---

[*] Neph, "Wat3r," *The Nephew Soundtrack*, 2024.

> Yeah they used to doubt me say I would never get it
> Used to say I'd be stretched or I'd be getting visits*

The screams grow closer and louder—I open my eyes.

"Oh my God!" I hear over and over. It's your mom and Grandma Beverly and they are all standing up, screaming, and crying. I close my eyes and listen to the cries.

> Unc told me to go get it, ngh u gifted
> I had to listen, I'm on a mission
> I know I'm here for a reason
> I got a purpose, gotta fulfil it†

"Hezekiah!" I hear Grandma Beverly say through tears. "Go and tell Hezekiah, 'This is what the Lord God of your ancestor David says: I have heard your prayer; I have seen your tears . . .'" I open my eyes, this time I notice Dr. Walker among them. He's not talking or explaining like usual, but listening.

Grandma Beverly continues, smiling now, "And God said, I am going to add years to your life. And I will rescue you and this city . . . Did he do it?" Everyone starts clapping and hugging like church. Now I can't close my eyes and I start to process what's going on.

You made it, Nephew, you fought, you rumbled that, and you rose.

---

*† Neph, "Believe," *The Nephew Soundtrack*, 2024.

Dr. Walker says he's never seen anything like it. Says it can only be described as some kind of "miracle" and lets a small, baffled grin slip out. Grandma Beverly invites him to Macedonia this Sunday.

I walk in and here you are, stunning and strong, a living miracle. You are awake, in pain but alert, and smile in a room full of love. I stare at you and you look just like that famous oil painting of that radiant black man in white linen, *The Moorish Chief*, by Eduard Charlemont.

You look at me—right in the eyes—and manage a smile and a nod.

You are scheduled to walk—walk!—out of the hospital. I will be walking beside you as you leave and you continue on your journey as an artist and walking miracle.

"I'm good," you assure the room.

"Boy, you're more than good. You're blessed, child! Hallelujah!" Grandma Beverly jumps in. "Didn't I tell you? Didn't I tell you?"

"You definitely did," I give her *her* flowers. My tears run like little sprinters down my face. It's surreal.

As I look at your body, patches over holes in your brown body, I remember Rumi's words:

The wound is the place where light enters you.

Let the light enter you, Nephew.

Nephew, the fire on Pearl Street changes Uzi's life.

I send Uzi your music, all tracks, everything that's on the drive. I hope you don't mind, but I believe, like Pearl Street, your "fire" has the power to change his life, too.

"It's never too late" is still the song.

# 28 / A Hundred Proof

Voice Message, September 22, 2021
From: Daahoud "Uzi" Jackson Asante
To: Nasir "Neph" Hassan Allen-Asante

Yo, Nas, What's up bro?

It's your father, yahmean.

Just hitting you up bro, I heard your music man, and, you
know, what can I say?

Your energy, your flow, your spirit, I see it.

Baby bro sent me the Instagram videos and the links and I'm
just looking at you like damn, yahmean, like, I'm really, really
feeling what you doing. Your whole style, your whole steez, your
whole ghost man. I'm very proud, man. You're super talented,
nahmean.

I was going to text you but I felt that was mad disrespectful,
you a grown man now. It was like, I ain't wanna say a lot of cliché
shit, apologizing for things that I made conscious decisions of

doing and acting like that wasn't what I wanted to do at that
particular time in my life, ya feel me.

Very proud of you, bro. Baby bro talks such good about you.
Bigs you up. Talks about how intelligent you are, you a deep boy.
Yeah, I'm definitely proud. I look at your music and I'm like he
got it. You keep on the wave and you gonna go on to big things.

I can't change the past, but I can definitely, nahmean, have
an influence on the future with me and you and an open line of
communication. I know you got some things to say and you feel
certain types of ways. That's all official and I'm not going to act
like that not a real thing.

But I did want to reach out to you and just tell you that I
look at you, you are from me and your mother, and I'm proud
of you. Your shit is thorough. I rap. He told me he played my
music for you and you was feeling that shit and I appreciate
that, nahmean, ya pop ain't no cornball boy. I'm official with
that rap shit.

Neither here nor there, I really would like to get to the point
where me and you can just fall back and rap and build on a
relationship in some form or fashion, feel me. I got you. If you
need anything, you can hit me up, I got you.

I was a young boy back in the day, and you know, I'm an OG
now, so I'm a whole completely different person. And um, I'm
glad you ain't doing one thousand years up top. That you still
out here, and you surviving, you been through a lot, and I want
to talk to you about all that. I don't want to disrespect you as

a grown man by trying to act like, you know . . . it's hard to explain . . . I was telling my brother . . .

It's easy to write or rhyme, but it's hard to talk to somebody that you know that got love for you and you got love for them, but it's a lot of issues in between, like this is real-life shit, like you my son, and you don't know me and I don't really know you.

It's only right for us to have some type of rapport with either, whether it be superficial on some what's up, what's up type . . . or we become friends. Whatever it might be, I want to tell you that I look at you, I seen you, I heard your music, I seen your ghost on the Instagram videos and I really think you got an energy that can take you a long way bro. I been around a lot of nghs and I been through a lot of shit just like you. And you been through maybe more shit than me on certain levels, and I wanna build with you on that, like damn how this go down, how that go down? But I know you a grown man and I don't want to disrespect you and act like this is just some simple shit and I can just come at you and be like yea yea, hit me up.

It's not like that.

I come at you with all respect, and all humbleness, as your father.

I'm just glad you was feeling my shit and I was feeling your shit and maybe that's the conduit for me and you to have a line of communication.

I know it ain't gonna be no overnight shit, I know you got . . .
you feel some type of way. I'm not going to take that away from
you. That what it is and I realize that.

I'm here. I ain't wanna text you. Like, the words ain't gon . . .
I fuck around and write a whole eighteen pages of text, like who
the fuck reading that—feel me?

I'm fucking with your shit. You that boy! I heard Face
Money did the video for you. I'm looking forward to seeing
that shit cause Face my man, that's my young boy. He told my
brother that you was a leader and that's good talk. I like that
type talk . . . that's the energy that's gonna take you a long way.
And make sure you channel that shit to . . . I'm not tryna tell
you what to do and blazay blah. You feel me? I got mad love for
you bro, whether you know it or not. It's that type time, we live
in that type world where we have to be around people that's of
our cloth, of right mind and right knowledge.

Regardless you are my son and I am your father and there's no
reason on this earth why we can't have some type of relationship
on a positive level.

I love you, boy, holla at me.

A CELEBRATION OF THE LIFE OF
*Dr. Kariamu Welsh*

Thursday October 28, 2021 11:00 AM

New Covenant Church of Philadelphia
7500 Germantown Ave. Philadelphia, PA 19119

Executive Pastor Bob Oliver
New Covenant Church
Founding Pastors
Bishop C. Milton Grannum
Ed.D., D.Min., Ph.D.
Rev. Hyacinth Bobb Grannum, D.D.

**PROGRAM**

OFFICIANT: Rev. Andrew Grannum

MUSICAL PRELUDE: Rev. Kevin Lawrence

PROCESSIONAL: Kariamu & Company

OPENING PRAYER: Rev. Andrew Grannum

SPECIAL MUSIC: Congregational Hymn from New Covenant
Church Worship and Music Arts with Rev. Kevin Lawrence

SPECIAL DANCE: Kariamu & Company, "Traditions,"
choreographed by C. Kemal Nance

SCRIPTURE: Old Testament: Psalm 23:1–4 New Testament: John 14:1–6

ACKNOWLEDGEMENTS, CONDOLENCES &
RESOLUTIONS: Kariana Smith

REMARKS: Dr. Kemal C. Nance and Dr. Indira Etwaroo

FAMILY TRIBUTE: Daahoud Asante Nikia
Morene Ahmed Artis MK Asante

MUSICAL SELECTION: New Covenant Church Worship
and Music Arts with Rev. Kevin Lawrence

OBITUARY:

Kariamu Welsh, age 72, made her transition peacefully in the early morning of Tuesday, October 12, 2021 at her home in Chapel Hill, North Carolina. She was born September 22, 1949, in Thomasville, North Carolina to Ruth Hoover. She moved with her mother to Brooklyn, New York, where she attended the public schools and graduated from Franklin K. Lane High School in 1967.

She went to college at SUNY Buffalo, where she majored in English. In 1970, she created her legendary dance technique, Umfundalai. Kariamu led her colleagues in creating the Black Dance Workshop, where they trained dancers and performed nationally. In 1974, she gave birth to her first son, Daahoud, in Buffalo. In 1979, the Black Dance Workshop became The Institute for Positive Thought with dance, martial arts, and an African and African American art gallery.

Kariamu was awarded a Fulbright in 1980 and moved to Zimbabwe. In Zimbabwe, she founded the country's National Dance Company and continued to teach Umfundalai. She married Molefi Kete Asante and gave birth to her second son, MK, in 1981 in Harare, Zimbabwe.

Upon returning to the United States, Kariamu received her doctorate from New York University. She was a full professor in African American Studies and later a full professor, chairperson, and professor emerita in the Department of Music and Dance at Temple University. She was generous with her time and spent countless hours mentoring and advising students.

She authored and edited the books *A Guide To African and African-American Art* (1980); *African Culture: Contributions in Afro-American and African Studies* (1985); *African Culture: The Rhythms of Unity* (1989); *The African Aesthetic: Keeper of the Traditions* (1993); *African Dance: An Artistic, Historical and Philosophical Inquiry* (1995); *Zimbabwe Dance: Rhythmic Forces, Ancestral Voices, an Aesthetic Analysis* (2000); *Umfundalai: An African Dance Technique* (2000); *African Dance - World of Dance* (2010); *Iwe Illanan: A Umfundalai Teacher's Handbook* (2017); and *Hot Feet and Social Change: African Dance and Diaspora Communities* (2019).

Kariamu received numerous grants and awards, including a National Endowment for the Arts Choreography fellowship, a Creative Public Service Award of New York, a Pew Fellowship, a Simon Guggenheim Fellowship, a Pennsylvania Council on the Arts grant, and three Fulbright Senior Scholar Awards.

Known affectionally as "Mama K," "Nna," or "Aunt Kari" by so many, Kariamu was loving, kind, generous, and had exceptionally high standards for herself and others. With an extraordinary eye for detail, she loved fine art, high fashion, architectural marvels, and interior design. A true intellectual, she read four newspapers per day, completed the *New York Times* crossword puzzle daily, and watched *Jeopardy!* nightly. She read a minimum of one novel per week and was a fierce Scrabble player.

Left to honor her are her mother, Ruth Hoover; siblings Sylvia Artis and William Hoover; sons Daahoud Jackson Asante and MK Asante; grandchildren Nasir Hassan Allen-Asante, Fukai Asante, Aion Asante, Akira Asante, Nova Asante, Akila Asante; dozens of nieces, nephews, and cousins; hundreds of students, master teachers of Umfundalai, and colleagues.

Kariamu's family would like to extend gratitude to all the loved ones who made her life joyous. A special thank-you to all who came to Chapel Hill to make her last days pleasant and remarkable. A special thank-you to her caregivers and neighbors in Chapel Hill. A special thank-you to her dancers and the Umfundalai community. In lieu of flowers, donations can be made to the Multiple Systems Atrophy Coalition in Kariamu's name.

Just like moons and like suns,
With the certainty of tides,
Just like hopes springing high,
Still I'll rise.

—MAYA ANGELOU

# 29 / The Color of Love

A lot of firsts today. This is the first time Uzi and Nasir have been in the same room. This is the first time Nasir's mom and dad have seen each other since conception. This is my first time in our old next door neighbor's church. This is my first time seeing Sam and Andy ("The Grannums"), my childhood friends and next door neighbors, as pastors. This is the first time I've ever cried in front of my kids.

This is the first time I hear my brother give a speech in public. The last time I saw him with a microphone, we were also together on the stage, at S.O.B.'s in New York, performing with Talib Kweli on MLK's Birthday. Clean, strong, towering, Uzi fights a storm of tears as he approaches the podium. He's sharp in a jet-black suit crowned in a fedora with a blood-red under brim. He speaks through a COVID-19 mask:

My dearest mother, our mother, our sister.

Our mentor, our Queen.

I find it very difficult to find the words to summarize the force called my mother.

How do you describe light? It's akin to describing color to someone who cannot see. So I'll try my best.

Such a vast and prolific life, such an impactful life. Everyone here has been touched by her in some way or form, and that will resonate with you throughout your whole lives.

My mother was a color. Vibrant, alive, beautiful, a patina of wisdom. And the canvas that is her life *is* and *was* a masterpiece.

So today, let's marvel at that masterpiece and appreciate it for the art that she is and will forever be.

My mother lived a full, accomplished, happy life. She did what most of us wish we could do: wake up with a true passion and be able to do that every day until your last day. And that deserves the ultimate respect.

I think back to when I was five or six, in upstate New York, just me and my mom, sitting in the Howard Johnson's. And I would hear that quiet clink of her spoon against her coffee cup. And that's a sound I still love to this day because of my mother. And I remember looking at her, my young self, and thinking she was the most beautiful woman in the world.

I truly thought she was a superhero. I knew she would protect me, and I knew she would always be there for me, and not one day, not even today, did she ever let me down.

She was a Queen, and by the grace of God, I was lucky enough to be her son.

They say when an elder passes, you lose a library, and I think we all understand this quote. But I will say that my mother was generous with the volumes of her library, and she gave each of us a personalized volume that is special to us. So today I ask you to refer to it as much as possible and speak the teachings and speak the lessons, and let the legacy live on, because the library is not gone, it's here with all of us, and we all possess a one of one, a one of a kind.

My mother has laced us with her tapestry and engulfed us in

vibrance and beauty and knowledge and wisdom. It is our duty today to celebrate her and remember her, and to not let her spirit die.

And once again, like I said before, I just feel incredibly blessed that I was lucky enough to be her son.

# Afterword

## Glad at You
### By Nasir aka Neph

But I ain't mad at you
Matter fact I'm glad at you

Blame yourself if I said I don't never need you
I was trying to reach out to you but ain't never reach you

When I was a buck I used to cry about it
Wasn't cool, I was confused, used to ask my mom about it

Now that I'm older I be thinking it was for the better
On my shoulder, had a chip, huh, under that sweater

Then I got shot my mom's told me you was tryna talk to me
But I don't wanna talk to you

Had to almost die for you to reach out to me, dog, that's crazy
Had to almost die, you ain't been worried 'bout me since a baby

But I ain't mad at you, matter fact I'm glad at you

Cause in these streets it made me go harder, it made me who I am
Still learning to be a man, matter fact, I am the man, damn

You told me you appreciate me not tripping at Nna funeral
Who you think I am?

She told me that us talking trying build would help her die in peace
Wasn't for her then I probably wouldn't have did it
Wasn't for her then this message I wouldn't send it

And you told me I can hit you if I need anything
To be honest, dog, I'm cool, man, I don't need anything
Man, I don't need . . .

And you got another child that you take care of
But I don't hold that against him if I see him give him bear hugs

Felt the same way since fourteen, nothing more but this a shoulder shrug
That's how I feel about it, ain't gonna lie, gotta be real about it

It only made it worse it's like a spitting image when you was a buck
When I was young, to know you, something I wanted so much

Ma stayed around him, she never wanted for much

Pour my feelings out, it's pain in this cup

# Asante Sana (Thank You)

To the Most High and the ancestors.

To Grandma Ruth, Nna, and Dad.

To Aion, Nova, Akira, Akila, and Wonderful.

To Nasir and Fukai.

To Uzi and Eka.

To Bianca and Beverly.

To Aunt Sylvia, Aunt Rosina, Ana, Ahmed, Nikia, Chris, Kariana, Mekhai, and all my family.

To Jan Miller and the team at Dupree Miller.

To Abby West, Makayla Tabron, Tracy Sherrod, and the team at Amistad/HarperCollins.

To Jeff Whitney and the team at the Sports & Entertainment Group.

To Kerri, Jen, and Melissa.

To Sanaa.

To Jon, Allen, Jordan, Sundiata, Joanna, Ben, Marquita, Kelene, Ari, Lee, Ta'Nai, Tejuan, Ace, Kota the Friend, Keith, Alesia, Sessi, Rico, Tobo, Ishe, Miete, Suzuko, Mama Starla, Daniel, Derek, Val, Shaness, Indira, Talib, Sam and Andy, Shakur, Nakia, Mez, and Kenny.

To Dustin Felder, rest in peace.

To uncle Melvin, rest in peace.

# About the Author

MK ASANTE is an award-winning filmmaker, recording artist, distinguished professor, and the bestselling author of *Buck: A Memoir*. He studied at SOAS University of London, earned a BA from Lafayette College, and an MFA from the UCLA School of Theater, Film, and Television.

He is the founder of Wonderful Sound Studios, a creative studio whose work has reached hundreds of millions of viewers. Asante cowrote the 2021 NBA Finals broadcast opens on ABC, directed by Academy Award–winning director Spike Lee. He wrote the official NFL Monday Night Football anthem, "In the Air Tonight," performed by Grammy-winning artist Chris Stapleton, Julie Blackman Santana, and Snoop Dogg.

He has toured in over fifty countries and was awarded the key to the city of Dallas, Texas. He is featured in *A Changing America*, a permanent video exhibit at the Smithsonian National Museum of African American History and Culture.

Asante has lectured at Harvard, Yale, and the British Library, and he was a Distinguished Professor-in-Residence at MICA Business School in Gujarat, India. He is currently a professor at Morgan State University, where he is the recipient of the Distinguished Achievement Award.